No Longer Property of
Phillips Memorial Library

ROMAN EDUCATION

ROMAN

EDUCATION

FROM CICERO TO QUINTILIAN

BY

AUBREY GWYNN

S.J.

New York
RUSSELL & RUSSELL
1964

FIRST PUBLISHED IN 1926
REISSUED, 1964, BY RUSSELL & RUSSELL, INC.
L. C. CATALOG CARD NO: 64—13935

PRINTED IN THE UNITED STATES OF AMERICA

PATRI MEO

FILIVS

PREFACE

THIS book is, though indirectly, the result of work begun ten years ago for the degree of M.A. in the National University of Ireland. At the suggestion of Rev. Dr. T. Corcoran, S.J., Professor of Education at University College, Dublin, I chose as a subject for research work the history of Roman education under the Empire and presented a thesis on that subject in the autumn of 1915. Thanks to a Travelling Studentship awarded me by the National University in that year, I was able to continue my studies for two years at Oxford, and I have since given what time I could spare from other work—part of it as student, part of it as teacher—to reading whatever might throw light on the general history of Graeco-Roman education. In the summer of 1919 I was awarded the degree of B.Litt. by the University of Oxford for a thesis entitled *Roman Education under the Empire*, in which I developed the ideas already set forth in my earlier thesis, adding a considerable body of new material. Since then I have worked mainly on the general principles which underlie all Greek and Roman theories of education, and have thought it best to publish separately the results of my inquiry into this more theoretical aspect of my subject, reserving for a later volume the history of the Roman schools under the Empire.

My thanks are due to the many kind friends who have helped me in one way or another; to my professors at University College, Dublin, without whose help and encouragement this book would never have been written; to Dr. L. C. Purser of Trinity College, Dublin, who gave me welcome advice at the beginning of my studies; to my tutors at Oxford, especially to Mr. J. G. C. Anderson of Christ Church; and to the Delegates of the Clarendon Press for undertaking the publication of this book.

A. G.

March 1925.

NOTE

A list of the modern works which I have consulted will be found at the end of this volume. For convenience of reference I have quoted works included in this Bibliography by the name of the author only, with the addition of a short title where there is more than one work by the same author. As a rule I have quoted the ancient authorities according to the Teubner editions; most of the authors whom I have used are not easily accessible in any other edition.

TABLE OF CONTENTS

I

EARLY ROMAN TRADITIONS

'Moribus antiquis res stat Romana virisque.' ENNIUS.

CICERO has devoted the fourth book of his *de Re publica* to an elaborate contrast between Greek and Roman political ideals. Most of the book is now lost, but what remains is of capital importance. After a brief enumeration of some characteristic Roman institutions, Scipio, who is Cicero's mouthpiece in the dialogue, begins his praise of the Roman state.

'Let us now turn our attention to other wise provisions made with a view to maintaining the prosperity and virtue of the commonwealth. For that is the primary purpose of all civil society towards which the state should help men, partly by its institutions, partly by its laws. Now first as to the education of free-born citizens. This is a problem on which the Greeks have wasted much endeavour: but our institutions are opposed to any detailed universal system of public education, obligatory by law. In fact my guest, Polybius, maintains that this is the one point on which our institutions can be accused of negligence.'[1]

Here the fragment breaks off, and the passage in Polybius to which Cicero refers—most probably a portion of the Greek historian's account of Roman institutions in his sixth book—is no longer extant. But the allusion thus made to a judgement passed by

[1] Cic. *de Rep.* iv. 3.

the most competent Greek critic of Roman history, and the fact that Cicero, the most competent Roman interpreter of Greek civilization, expressly rejects that judgement, indicate a suggestive line of inquiry. Why should Polybius have singled out this neglect of public education as the one fault in Roman institutions ? And why should Cicero have been at pains (for Scipio was evidently made to answer the criticism which he quotes) not merely to refute the Greek historian's opinion, but even to select Roman methods of education as the starting-point for his eulogy of Roman institutions ? Were both men aware of an essential difference between Greek and Roman educational ideals ?

Little is known of early Roman education, but one fact is certain. As in every other department of Roman social life, the centre round which all turned was the family ; and in particular that most Roman institution, the *patria potestas.* 'The right of dominion', says Gaius, 'which we have over our children is peculiar to the citizens of Rome, nor is there any race of men who have a dominion over their children similar to ours.'[1] Roman law allowed the father a dominion over his children hardly less absolute than the dominion exercised over slaves. When the child was born the father was free to accept him as a member of the *familia* or to reject him as unfit ; in poorer circles, at least, the practice of exposing infants was common and the foundling that survived could be picked up by the first-comer,

[1] Gaius, i. 55 ; *Inst.* i. 9, 2 ; *Digest,* i. 6, 3.

retained as his slave or sold to the highest bidder. Nor was this the only possibility of slavery for the Roman child. In theory, at least, a Roman father could sell an unmarried child into slavery at will, as he could also punish him by condemning him to work on his fields among the farm-hands.

How far these rights were put into practice is disputed;[1] their legality is certain. And a Roman father had the supreme right of condemning his son to death, subject only to the moral obligation of holding a family council before passing this final sentence. More practical were the laws which governed the holding of property. Here again the patriarchal system was in full force. The son had no personal property as distinct from his father, and whatever goods he acquired during his father's life-time were legally the property of the *paterfamilias*: money allowed him for his personal use could be revoked by the father at will. The one legal difference between the son and the slave was the right to inherit. When the father died, the son, hitherto regarded in law as co-proprietor, but without use, of his father's property, entered upon rights which had been in abeyance during his father's lifetime. Finally, apart from a privilege granted to the holders of certain priestly offices, this *patria potestas* was extinguished only by death: neither marriage nor high office in the state made the son independent of his father within the sphere of private life. Adoption

[1] Blümner, p. 302; Beauchet in Daremberg-Saglio, iv, pp. 344 foll.

was merely the transference of *patria potestas* from one parent to the other.

As might be expected in a society which held paternal authority in such honour, a Roman boy's education consisted almost entirely in daily familiar intercourse with his parents and in the close imitation of his father's conduct. Tacitus has left a picture of this traditional home-education which, though idealized by the historian's imagination, is no doubt true to its essential spirit.

> 'Of old our children were born of chaste parents and were reared, not in the chamber of some hired nurse, but in the lap or at the breast of their mother, whose chief glory was thus to stay at home and be the servant of her children. Choice was made of some matron from among the family's relatives, to whom were entrusted all the children of the same household. Of well-proved virtue, her influence was such that none dared utter before her an unseemly word or venture on an unbecoming action. Her presence, commanding awe and reverence, was there to check the children not merely at their lessons and serious duties, but even during their games and recreations. Thus, tradition tells us, did Cornelia train the Gracchi; Aurelia, Julius Caesar; Atia, Augustus for future empire. And the aim of all this stern formation was that whilst the child's character was still fresh and open and unspoiled by wrong, he should be taught to embrace the practice of virtue with all his heart; and that whether destined to be soldier, jurist or orator, his whole energies should be solely devoted to duty.'[1]

Once the first years of childhood were past, the mother's place in the boy's education was taken by her husband, and a companionship began between father and son for which it is hard to find a parallel outside Roman society. School-life was reduced to

[1] Tac. *Dial.* 28; see also Pliny, *Epp.* vii. 24.

a minimum, where it existed at all. Frequently the father took over in person the responsibility of giving his son whatever little book-learning was required for ordinary Roman life. 'Every child had his father for schoolmaster', says Pliny of these early times;[1] and the practice is expressly affirmed by Plutarch of the elder Cato and Aemilius Paulus.[2] But these elementary lessons were the least part of the boy's education. Constantly at his father's side and with few other companions, he learnt to see in his parent the living representative of Roman tradition, the personification of Roman authority. At home he worked with his father on the farm, like the Sabine 'soldier-peasants' of Horace's ode;[3] or like the elder Cato who 'spent all his youth in habits of frugality and hardship and industry, tilling the fields, ploughing up Sabine rocks and stones, or sowing the land for harvest'.[4] On festival days he acted as acolyte to his father in all the religious ceremonies which centred round the Roman hearth; or accompanied him as guest at the house of friends, serving his elders at table and singing with others of his own age the ballads of early Roman literature.[5] When there was a meeting of the assembly in the forum, he was there to listen to the public debates; and, if his father was a senator, he was allowed by special privilege—at least in the early days of the

[1] Pliny, *Epp.* viii. 14, 6. [2] Plut. *Cato maior*, 20; *Aemil.* 6.
[3] Hor. *Carm.* iii. 6, 37 foll. [4] Cato *apud* Fest. 281 a, 21.
[5] Plut. *Qu. Rom.* 33; Varro *apud* Non. 77, 3 (=i, p. 107, Lindsay).

Republic—to go with him to the senate-house, 'sitting near the door, and learning both from what he heard and what he saw '.[1]

According to primitive Roman custom this strictly parental training was continued until the boy was sixteen or seventeen years old.[2] It was ended only by the formal assumption of the *toga virilis*, when the boy, now recognized as a Roman citizen, entered upon his first experiences of active military service. Later a custom was introduced which served as a prolongation of this parental training. Once the home-education was judged to have been sufficient, the boy laid aside his *praetexta* for the *toga virilis*, often when he was only thirteen or fourteen years old. He was then taken by his father to some distinguished citizen and bidden learn from him the lessons of political oratory and statecraft which the home-circle was too limited to give.[3] As Cicero puts it, speaking of his own experience, 'I was taken by my father to Scaevola, and bidden as far as possible never leave his side '.[4] This sort of apprenticeship to public life—*tirocinium fori*, as it was called by the Romans themselves—lasted for a year, and was regarded as a transitional stage between the strict discipline of the home-circle and the freedom of public life as a Roman citizen.[5] Those who intended to devote themselves to a military career passed through a similar appren-

[1] Pliny, *Epp.* viii. 14, 4 ; Gell. i. 23, 4.
[2] Marquardt, i, pp. 123–34.
[3] Tac. *Dial.* 34 ; Warde Fowler, *Social Life*, pp. 191 foll.
[4] Cic. *de Am.* 1 ; see below, p. 64.
[5] Cic. *pro Cael.* 11.

ticeship to active service (*tirocinium militiae*), under the care of some experienced officer;[1] for these customs belong to a period when military service was no longer compulsory. And even when this year of apprenticeship was over, and the young citizen or officer had begun to play his part in the service of the state, his private life was still subject to parental authority. For the Roman *patria potestas* ended only with the parent's death, and citizens of the highest standing owed their parents an obedience which disconcerts our modern opinions, as of old it disconcerted Greek critics of Roman institutions.[2] *Moribus antiquis res stat Romana virisque*: the extent of a Roman parent's influence on the education of his children gives fuller meaning to this reverence for the living traditions of Roman greatness.

Early Roman education was thus little concerned with the development of intellectual attainments. Its main object was to form that spirit of self-restraint and filial submission which Roman feeling demanded of the young;[3] its chief merit was that it fostered a reverence for childhood which made every boy and girl an object of almost religious veneration.[4] But it would be a mistake to remain blind to the faults of the system. Judged by intellectual standards, Roman education was essentially

[1] Cic. *apud* Serv. *in Aen.* v. 546; Marquardt, i, p. 133.
[2] Dion. Hal. *Ant. Rom.* ii. 26, 2; 27, 1.
[3] Cic. *de Off.* ii. 46.
[4] See Warde Fowler's article in *Roman Essays*, pp. 42 foll.

utilitarian. Cicero notes a characteristic example. Greek thinkers had always taken a keen interest in theoretical geometry; but the Romans never troubled to learn more of the science than was necessary for the practical work of land-measurement.[1] And Horace's satire on the utilitarian aim of Roman mathematics is too familiar to need quotation.[2] The same spirit of conservative utilitarianism is manifest in the whole character of early Roman education: it influenced the training of both body and mind. Athletics, if we take the word in the sense of all healthy physical exercise, played a large part in the daily life of a Roman boy. Running, riding, boxing, wrestling, swimming, hunting, the use of arms and hard work in the fields:[3] all these formed part of his regular education, and Roman conservatives like Virgil and Horace were staunch upholders of the national tradition.[4] Varro, who believed in letting boys rough it when they were young,[5] has left an interesting description of his own boyhood. He had only one tunic and toga, wore sandals without any covering for his legs, rode his horse bare-backed, was seldom allowed a bath, and even less frequently a good dinner.[6] But the scientific training of an ideal harmony of mind and body as practised by the Greeks was unknown to

[1] Cic. *Tusc.* i. 5. [2] Hor. *Ars poet.* 325 foll.

[3] Plut. *Cato maior*, 20; Blümner, p. 329.

[4] Virg. *Aen.* vii. 160 foll.; ix. 603 foll.; Hor. *Carm.* i. 8; iii. 6; 24.

[5] Varro *apud* Non. 520, 24 (=iii, p. 837, Lindsay); Gell. iv. 19.

[6] Varro *apud* Non. 108, 24 (=i, p. 155, Lindsay).

Roman tradition, and Roman society never fully accepted the Greek athletic ideal. Even the younger Scipio, the greatest phil-Hellene of his day, found much that was harmful and absurd in the traditions of the Greek gymnasia;[1] and Cato was open in his hostility.[2] Plutarch gives some curious details as to the latter's theory of education in the twentieth chapter of his *Life of Cato*. But the whole chapter is so admirable in itself, and so entirely characteristic of Roman educational ideals, that it deserves to be quoted in full.

'Cato was a good father and an honourable husband. In the management of his household he showed unusual ability, and was far from treating such questions as of little or secondary importance; so that I think it worth while to give some details as to his success in these matters. He married a wife of good family rather than of great fortune, judging that, whilst both good birth and wealth make for pride and seriousness, women of noble family, owing to their dread of shame, are more obedient to their husbands in all questions of good conduct. He used to say that a man who struck his wife or his child was laying hands on the most holy of sacred things; that it was a greater honour to be a good husband than a distinguished senator; and that nothing was more admirable in old Socrates than that he lived in peace and quiet with a difficult wife and half-witted children. When his son was born, no duty (save perhaps some public function) was so pressing as to prevent him from being present when his wife bathed the child and wrapped it in its swaddling-clothes. His wife suckled the child with her own milk, and would often give her breast to the children of her slaves, so as to gain their affection for her son by treating them as his brothers. As soon as the boy was able to learn, Cato took him personally in charge and taught him his letters, although he owned an accomplished slave, named Chilon, who was a schoolmaster and gave lessons

[1] Cic. *de Rep.* iv. 4; *Tusc.* iv. 70. [2] Plut. *Cato maior*, 3.

to many boys. But Cato, to use his own words, would not have a slave abuse his son nor perhaps pull his ears for being slow at his lessons ; nor would he have his boy owe a slave so precious a gift as learning. So he made himself the boy's schoolmaster, just as he taught him the laws of Rome and bodily exercises ; not merely to throw the javelin, to fight in armour or to ride, but also to use his fists in boxing, to bear heat and cold, and to swim against the currents and eddies of a river. And he tells us himself that he wrote books of history with his own hand and in large characters, so that his son might be able even at home to become acquainted with his country's past ; that he was as careful to avoid all indecent conversation in his son's presence as he would have been in presence of the Vestal virgins ; and that he never bathed with him. This last point seems to have been a Roman custom, for even fathers-in-law were careful not to bathe with their sons-in-law to avoid the necessity of stripping naked before them ; but later, when the Romans had learnt from the Greeks the custom of appearing naked, they actually taught the Greeks to do so before women. When Cato had thus taken every pains to fashion his son, like an excellent work, to virtue, finding that his good will was beyond reproach and that he was naturally docile and obedient, but that his body was too delicate for hardship, he relaxed the excessive rigour and austerity of this regime. And in spite of weak health the lad proved himself a true man in the field, winning great distinction in the battle which Aemilius Paulus fought against Perseus. It was here that he lost his sword, which was struck from his grasp by a blow or simply slipped owing to the moisture of his hand. Grieved at this loss the boy turned to some of his comrades who were about him, took them with him, and again charged the enemy. Much hard fighting was needed to clear the spot, but at last he found his sword amid a heap of arms and dead bodies, friend and foe piled up together. His general Paulus was delighted with the boy when he heard of the deed, and Cato himself wrote his son a letter which is still extant, giving him high praise for the honourable zeal he had shown in thus winning back his sword. Later the young man married Tertia, the daughter of Paulus and Scipio's sister, and his admission to this noble family was due as much to his own merits as to the merits of his father. So that Cato's care for his son had its fitting reward.'

Comment on such a passage is unnecessary. However rigid its ethical standard, however narrow its intellectual horizon, the austere morality which Cato here personifies compels admiration. Ennius was right: these traditions and these men were the guarantee of Roman greatness.

II

GREEK AND ROMAN EDUCATIONAL IDEALS

'Considerate nunc . . . disciplinam puerilem ingenuis ; in qua Graeci multum frustra laboraverunt.' Cic. *de Rep.* iv. 3.

PLUTARCH was not the first Greek to feel the impressive grandeur of Roman educational ideals. Polybius—in spite of the criticism which Cicero quotes—renders generous homage to the ethical value of Roman family traditions. National custom required that at the funeral of a Roman citizen life-size statues of former members of the family should be carried in solemn procession through the forum, adorned with all the insignia of their rank. After the procession a panegyric was pronounced on the dead man's virtues and achievements, and the glories of his ancestors. Polybius, who describes the scene at one of these public ceremonies, interrupts his narrative to note the effect of all this pageantry on an impressionable boy.

'It would not be easy', he says, 'to offer a fairer spectacle to an ambitious and generous boy. For who would not be moved to see the statues of men famous for their valour grouped together as though they were alive ? What fairer spectacle could there be than this ? And, best of all, the young are thus stimulated to bear all manner of hardship for the common weal, hoping thereby to gain the glory which is given to brave men.' [1]

Roman tradition—the *mos maiorum*, so prominent in Latin literature—has seldom been more justly praised.

[1] Polyb. vi. 53, 9–54, 3 (ed. Büttner-Wobst).

Why then did Polybius find fault with Roman methods of education ? His complaint that Romans neglected the problem of public education recalls an observation made by Aristotle two centuries earlier :

> 'It is only in the Spartan community, with a few other exceptions, that the lawgiver has paid attention to the problem of education. In most states such questions are ignored : every one lives the lord of his wife and children, like the Cyclops of old.' [1]

Possibly Aristotle would have been too shrewd an observer of moral forces to include Roman traditions in a criticism aimed directly at the customs of fourth-century Greece ; but Polybius was less wary. Greek political theory of the second century B.C. demanded that education should be controlled by public laws, and Polybius, though personal experience should have taught him better, missed the application of a theory in which he had been taught to believe. Roman statesmen sought a solution of these problems according to the genius of their race. Where Greek theorists put their faith in systematic law-making, the Romans obtained more permanent results by the slow development of custom : as Polybius puts it, 'they learnt from experience, choosing always the best', and thereby built up institutions which Polybius himself prefers to the institutions of any other state, because of their more perfect conformity with nature.[2] And the success achieved by this practical wisdom in general was notable in the sphere of education. The Roman

[1] Ar. *Eth. Nic.* x. 1180 a, 25 ; *Pol.* viii. 1337 a, 30.

[2] Polyb., vi. 10, 14 ; 4, 13 ; 9, 12 (ed. Büttner-Wobst).

father was free to educate his children as he pleased. 'Like the Cyclops of old', he was their lord, and the state made no attempt to restrict his freedom. But each family had its own tradition of family pride, its own record of public service; and the atmosphere of conservative custom thus created was for centuries a sufficient guarantee against novel experiments. Towards the end of the second century B.C., when individualist tendencies were making themselves felt, conservative statesmen appealed to the value of these traditions. Suetonius has preserved the text of an edict issued by the censors of 92 B.C., in opposition to the new tendencies.[1] One of its sentences runs as follows: 'Our ancestors were careful to determine what lessons their children were to learn, what schools they were to attend.' No one familiar with the spirit of early Roman education can doubt the truth of this statement. Yet no laws were in existence, prescribing this or that form of education, and Cicero's statement holds true: 'Our institutions are opposed to any detailed universal system of public education, obligatory by law.'[2]

By way of contrast with these early Roman traditions it may be helpful to quote in full a well-known passage of Plato's *Protagoras*, which expresses more clearly than any other passage in Greek literature certain fundamental ideas common to all Greek theories of education.

'Education and admonition', says Protagoras, 'commence in the first years of childhood, and last to the very end of life.

[1] Suet. *Rhet*. 1.

[2] Cic. *de Rep*. iv. 3.

Mother and nurse and father and tutor are quarrelling about the improvement of the child as soon as ever he is able to understand them ; he cannot say or do anything without their setting forth to him that this is just and that is unjust ; this is honourable and that is dishonourable ; this is holy, that is unholy ; do this and abstain from that. And if he obeys, well and good ; if not, he is straightened by threats and blows, like a piece of warped wood. At a later stage they send him to teachers, and enjoin them to see to his manners even more than to his reading and music ; and the teachers do as they are desired. And when the boy has learned his letters and is beginning to understand what is written, as before he understood only what was spoken, they put into his hands the works of great poets which he reads at school ; in these are contained many admonitions and many tales, and praises, and encomia of ancient famous men which he is required to learn by heart, in order that he may imitate or emulate them and desire to become like them. Then, again, the teachers of the lyre take similar care that their young disciple is temperate and gets into no mischief ; and when they have taught him the use of the lyre, they introduce him to the poems of other excellent poets, who are the lyric poets ; and these they set to music, and make their harmonies and rhythms quite familiar to the children's souls, in order that they may learn to be more gentle, and harmonious, and rhythmical, and so more fitted for speech and action ; for the life of man in every part has need of harmony and rhythm. Then they send them to the master of gymnastic, in order that their bodies may better minister to the virtuous mind, and that they may not be compelled through bodily weakness to play the coward in war or on any other occasion. This is what is done by those who have the means, and those who have the means are the rich ; their children begin education soonest and leave off latest. When they have done with masters, the state again compels them to learn the laws and live after the pattern which they furnish, and not after their own fancies ; and just as in learning to write, the writing-master first draws lines with a style for the use of the young beginner, and gives him the tablet and makes him follow the lines, so the city draws the laws, which were the invention of good lawgivers who were of old time ; these are given to the young man in order to guide him in his conduct, whether as ruler or ruled; and he who transgresses them is to be corrected or, in other words, called to account, which is a term used not only in your country, but also in many others. Now when there is all this care about virtue private and public, why, Socrates, do you still wonder and doubt whether virtue can be taught? Cease to wonder, for the opposite would be far more surprising.'[1]

Here is ethical idealism as noble as that which Plutarch attributes to the elder Cato; yet how different are the two pictures! On the one hand, an education which depends almost entirely on the silent forces of tradition, home-life, and example; on the other, a systematic training in this art followed by that art, until the child's mental and moral education is completed by enforced submission to the city's laws. And the history of Greek education, whether Athenian or Spartan, illustrates in detail this general contrast between Greek and Roman ideals. At Sparta boys were left in their mother's charge during the years of infancy; but from the age of seven they ceased by law to belong to their homes, and were incorporated in one or other of the famous 'divisions' and 'packs' characteristic of the Spartan system.[2] Here the boys were grouped together in companies of varying age, subjected to an iron discipline, made to feed together, play together, sleep together; and though they were also required from time to time to attend the men's clubs, where they sat at their father's feet and listened to the talk of their elders, it is plain that these well-organized and systematic

[1] Plato, *Protagoras*, 325–6 (tr. Jowett).
[2] Plut. *Lycurg.* 16; Freeman, pp. 11–34.

methods were the very opposite of Roman habits, which allowed for constant and intimate familiarity between father and son.

At Athens, though for very different reasons, the obstacles to parental influence were, if anything, greater than at Sparta. During infancy, the mother's influence on her children was inconsiderable, owing partly to the inferior position of women in Athenian households, partly to their excessive dependence on the service of slaves. Once the boy was of an age to begin his lessons, his mother's lack of higher education made itself felt, and national custom did not give her that authority over her children which was claimed and held by Roman matrons. Nor was the father's influence much greater. Always absent from his home, at the meeting of the Ecclesia or about his business, he had little time to devote to his son's education, and seems as a rule to have had even less interest.[1] For at Athens, as at Sparta, the education of the young was looked upon as a public rather than a private matter, and was entrusted exclusively to professional hands. It has been disputed whether or no attendance at school was obligatory by Athenian law.[2] Probably it was. At any rate school-attendance was universal in Attica, and the state intervened from an early period with regulations as to the age at which attendance was desirable, the hours of class, the conduct of pupils, and so forth.[3] An Athenian

[1] Girard, pp. 75 foll.

[2] Girard, pp. 32 foll.; Iwan-Müller, p. 166; Walden, pp. 58 foll.

[3] Aesch. *c. Tim.* 6–12; Isocr. *Areop.* 43–5.

citizen was thus always able to read and write, to count and sing and play the lyre. But this was the least characteristic result of Athenian education. Even in Sparta, as Plutarch tells us,[1] every citizen had these necessary elements of education, and at Rome, where the state made no attempt to regulate school-attendance, the number of illiterates was probably very small.[2] More characteristic of Athenian life was the general opinion that education—culture, or *παιδεία* to use the regular Athenian phrase—was an art, to be learnt in turn by each individual, and capable of raising him, according to the varying degree of his capacity and industry, above the common herd of men.

The most striking illustration of this fundamental difference between Greek and Roman habits of thought is to be found in the early history of schools in Greece and Rome. As far back as we can trace the history of Greek culture, schoolmasters appear as a regular feature of Greek social life. Achilles, the ideal type of heroic Achaean youth, is the pupil of Phoenix in the *Iliad,* of Chiron in later Greek tradition ; and the relation of tutor and pupil is evidently characteristic of early Greek feudalism.[3] The precise date at which regular public schools were formed in Ionia and on the Greek mainland cannot be determined ; but Athenian tradition attributed school-laws to Draco and Solon, and it is certain that schools were common in Athens at least as early as the sixth

[1] Plut. *Lycurg.* 16.
[2] Jullien, pp. 21 foll.
[3] Iwan-Müller, p. 155.

century B.C.[1] At Sparta they can be traced back to an earlier date. For the Spartan system of education, as known to us from later authorities, forms an essential part of the Lycurgean constitution; and there is nothing to distinguish this system of life in common, with its 'divisions', prefects and regular duties, from the principle of modern boarding schools.

In Rome, national legends—at least in their later hellenized form—suggest that schools were common from the first days of the city's history. Plutarch sends Romulus and Remus to school at Gabii,[2] and there are frequent allusions of this kind to schools in other stories of primitive Rome, most famous of all being the episode of Verginia.[3] Do these legendary tales represent any measure of historical truth, or do they simply reflect the social conditions of a later age? It is impossible to tell; but there is a passage in one of Plutarch's *Quaestiones Romanae* which requires notice.[4] 'The Romans', he says, 'were late in beginning to teach for payment, and the first of them to open a school of letters was Spurius Carvilius, a freedman of that Carvilius who was the first Roman to divorce his wife.' Carvilius was consul in 235 B.C.; so that his freedman's school belongs to the middle of the third century, and (if Plutarch's statement is literally true) schools were thus of comparatively recent origin in Rome. There are,

1 Aesch. *loc. cit.*; Plut. *Solon*, 1; Girard, pp. 38 foll.

2 Plut. *Rom.* 6.

3 Livy, iii. 44, 6; v. 27, 1; vi. 25, 9; Dion. Hal., *Ant. Rom.* xi. 28, 3.

4 Plut. *Qu. Rom.* 59; cf. Gell. iv. 3, 2; xvii. 21, 44.

however, good reasons for not taking Plutarch's statement literally. The knowledge of reading or writing was certainly common at a much earlier date in Roman history,[1] and Cicero mentions a custom which required that every Roman child should know the Twelve Tables by heart.[2] These facts suggest, though they do not prove, the existence of regular schools where children could be taught to read and write. Moreover, Plautus alludes more than once to scenes from school-life in passages which seem to be the reflection of ordinary Roman customs, not mere transcripts from his Greek originals.[3] Could schools have been so familiar a spectacle in the Roman society of his day if their origin was of such recent date as the passage already quoted suggests ?

It is not easy to reconcile the conflicting evidence of these authorities. One or two scholars have solved the problem by the simple rejection of Plutarch's statement.[4] But Plutarch is usually good authority, and the curiously precise nature of his information suggests that he is here following some well-informed source. A more probable interpretation has been put forward by a French scholar.[5] Many of our ancient authorities mention a custom according to which Roman schoolboys brought their masters presents on certain festival-days throughout the

[1] Mommsen, *History*, i, p. 281 ; ii, pp. 115 foll. (Eng. tr. 1894).

[2] Cic. *de Leg.* ii. 59.

[3] Plaut. *Bacch.* 420 foll. ; *Merc.* 303 ; *Pers.* 173.

[4] Blümner, p. 314.

[5] Jullien, pp. 26 foll. ; Wilkins, p. 23.

year, in particular on the feast of Minerva.[1] Assuming, as is natural enough, that this custom dates back to the origins of school life in Rome, Plutarch's words can be explained as due to a misunderstanding of the statement in his source. Spurius Carvilius may have been the first schoolmaster to charge a regular fee for his classes. This would imply that before his day schoolmasters were dependent on the generosity of their pupils' parents, just as Roman advocates under the Republic were always, in theory at least, dependent for their income on the generosity of their clients. One of the professors of literature mentioned by Suetonius in his *de Grammaticis* retained this method of payment by voluntary contributions until well on in the first century B.C.;[2] and the history of Irish hedge-schools is a reminder that a sound tradition of national education can exist for centuries without any form of permanent endowment or state-control.

But the whole status of the teaching class was lower in Rome than in any part of Greece. Alcibiades might box his schoolmaster's ears, but Greeks as a rule were almost subservient in their respect for the 'wise man', who could teach others how to be virtuous and clever. In Rome teachers were less fortunate, and the Greek tradition was slow in penetrating Roman society. Most of the 'illustrious' professors of literature and rhetoric, whose names have been recorded by Suetonius, were either slaves or freedmen. Their names, too (names now long

[1] Varro. *de Re rust.* iii. 3, 18; Ovid, *Fast.* iii. 815 foll.; Tert. *de Idol.* 10.

[2] Suet. *Gram.* 7.

since forgotten, with the exception of Orbilius) usually betray Greek origin, and the general reputation of Greek slaves in Rome can have done little to increase the respect of their pupils. One of them is said to have started life as a porter, chained to his master's door.[1] Another, Lutatius Daphnis, was sold for 700,000 sesterces, a record price on the Roman slave-market.[2] That was in the hey-day of Greek influence, when prices were running high, and Suetonius remarks that the figures these learned slaves commanded in the market were as high as the fees which their masters charged for their classes.[3] The inevitable consequence of this curious boom was a trade in the buying and selling of educated slaves. The practice was, of course, degrading for both pupils and professors, though we hear of some fortunate exceptions. Sulla, Pompey, Atticus, and Julius Caesar had each a professor among his clients,[4] and Curtius Nicias figures as a friend in Cicero's correspondence.[5] Another of these *grammatici* could boast that he had given Sallust the matter for his history and Pollio his style.[6] But that was later in the history of Roman education. Cato's attitude towards his slave Chilon was characteristic of the second century B.C.; and even the professors who were not slaves had no adequate social standing. Orbilius was a free man, and exceptionally learned;

[1] Suet. *Rhet.* 3.
[2] Suet. *Gram.* 3; Pliny, *N. H.* vii. 128.
[3] Suet. *Gram.* 3.
[4] *ibid.* 12; 15; 16; 7.
[5] Cic. *ad Fam.* ix. 10; Suet. *gram.* 14.
[6] Suet. *Gram.* 10.

and Horace made his name proverbial within a generation of his death. But he worked in extreme poverty all his life, and wrote a book on the way in which parents neglect to pay money due for the education of their sons.[1]

[1] *ibid.* 9.

III

FIRST GREEK TEACHERS IN ROME

'At vero nos, docti scilicet a Graecia, haec et a pueritia legimus et discimus: hanc eruditionem liberalem et doctrinam putamus.' Cic. *Tusc.* ii. 27.

THE contrast is extreme between the older tradition of Roman education and the new Graeco-Roman culture which was so soon to take its place. On the one side a tradition of family life and national custom, with no higher form of literary education than the elementary instruction necessary for life's work. On the other, an ideal of culture which included Greek literature, rhetoric, and philosophy, and was necessarily dependent on school instruction for the acquisition of this knowledge. The change was inevitable once Rome, hitherto the centre of a small group of Italian towns, became the metropolis of a world-empire. But the circumstances of the change were due to the influence of half a dozen distinguished Greeks who came to Rome during the second and third centuries B.C.

Livius Andronicus, the first Greek to write in Latin, and thereby the founder of Latin literature, came to Rome from Tarentum, probably in the year 272 B.C., and was active as teacher and writer until the end of the century.[1] Employed by his patrons

[1] Schanz, i. 1, pp. 56 foll.

as Latin and Greek tutor for their sons, he soon found the need of supplanting the Twelve Tables by a more literary Latin text-book. His translation of the Odyssey was the result: a work destined to remain a classic in Roman schools for at least two centuries.[1] Of the other early Latin poets Ennius is of special importance, not merely as a writer, but also as a teacher. An Italian by birth, he was Greek by education—'half-Greek' as Suetonius calls him; and he gave lessons at Rome in Greek and Latin literature.[2] But the whole character of his versatile literary activity shows that he was consciously working for the Hellenization of Roman society. That his influence in this direction was immense and lasting is plain from the numerous quotations of his verses which occur in later authors, above all in Cicero. Yet by a strange irony of fate, it was Cato the censor, later the most stubborn opponent of Greek culture, who brought the young poet to Rome from Sardinia in 204 B.C.[3] What were the old Roman's thoughts, one wonders, when Ennius died twenty-six years later, leaving behind him a vast body of Graeco-Roman poetry, and an influence which was only to grow stronger as generation followed generation in the new tendency towards Greek culture?

The very year in which Ennius died was marked by the arrival of another stranger, whose personal influence was hardly less important. Crates of

[1] Suet. *Gram.* 1; Hor. *Epp.* ii. 1, 69.
[2] Suet. *Gram.* 1; Schanz, i. 1, p. 111.
[3] Corn. Nepos, *Cato*, 1, 4; Jerome, *Chron.* a. 1777 (=240 B.C.).

Mallos, the most distinguished scholar of the Pergamene school, famous as a grammarian and a brilliant lecturer, came to Rome on an embassy from the royal family of Pergamon, most probably in 168 B.C.[1] An accident (he fell into one of the Roman drains and broke his leg) kept him for some weeks in Rome, and the ambassador turned his convalescence to good account by giving public lectures on Greek literature and grammar to any who might care to come. The effect of these lectures was enormous. Hitherto it had been possible for Romans interested in Greek literature to attend the classes of teachers like Livius Andronicus and Ennius, perhaps also Spurius Carvilius. But the lessons of these early schoolmasters had been confined to a few texts, and were of an elementary character. Now for the first time they heard the lectures of a cultivated scholar, and could form some idea of the erudition and discernment peculiar to Hellenistic literary criticism. There was also a personal interest in the lectures of Crates, owing to his lifelong controversy with the more famous Aristarchus of Alexandria. Aristarchus had formulated strict laws of linguistic formation, which were challenged by Crates and his school; and discussion was particularly hot as to the correct interpretation of certain Homeric forms. The followers of Aristarchus were known as the Analogists; Crates was the leader of the Anomalists, and his criticisms were as erudite as they were lively.[2] The

[1] Suet. *Gram.* 2; Schanz, i. 1, p. 329.

[2] Susemihl, ii, pp. 5 foll.; Sandys, i, pp. 156 foll.

controversy, then at its height, was undoubtedly discussed by Crates at Rome, and the double interest which he was thus able to give his teaching is plain from the history of early Roman scholarship. Greek methods of criticism are now for the first time applied to Latin literature. Critical editions of Naevius, Plautus, and Ennius begin to appear,[1] and the controversy between Analogists and Anomalists is hotly debated. L. Aelius Stilo, the first Roman grammarian, seems to have followed Crates in his Anomalist theory: later Julius Caesar himself wrote a famous treatise on behalf of the Analogists.[2]

Suetonius dates Roman interest in literary criticism and grammar from this visit of Crates to Rome: the year 168 B.C. is thus an important landmark in the history of Roman erudition. But a more important innovation in educational method belongs to the same period, though its date cannot be exactly determined. In 161 B.C. the senate passed a decree empowering the praetor to expel all teachers of philosophy and rhetoric from the city.[3] This is the first mention in Roman history of teachers who were later to dispute between themselves the claim to a monopoly of Roman higher education. How long they had been in Rome before the senate's decree is uncertain. A fragment of Ennius contains a casual reference to students of rhetoric; but the poem from which it is taken was copied from a Greek original, and it would be unsafe to infer that Ennius had in

[1] Schanz, i. 1, p. 329. [2] *ibid.*, p. 333. [3] Suet. *Rhet.* 1.

mind Roman students of rhetoric.[1] There is also a reference to the study of philosophy in one of his tragedies :

Philosophandum est, sed paucis ; nam omnino haud placet.[2]

The verse, which is quoted by Cicero and Gellius, suggests that Roman audiences were already familiar with Greek theories of higher education. Certain it is, at least, that the decree of 161 B.C. was without effect. As far as the teaching of rhetoric is concerned, the failure of the decree is plain from the whole history of early Roman oratory. Cicero's *Brutus* describes a development which is marked by a constant and increasing endeavour to model Roman prose according to the laws of Greek rhetoric and prose-rhythm : a sufficient proof of the existence and influence of Greek teachers. Sempronius Gracchus, father of the Gracchi, was able to deliver a Greek oration before a highly critical audience at Rhodes, probably in 164 B.C. ;[3] and his contemporary, Aemilius Paulus, father of the younger Scipio, was another accomplished orator. Paulus was also noted for the care he took to give his sons a Greek education.[4] Sempronius Gracchus died before he could take part in the education of his two sons, but his wife—the famous Cornelia, daughter of the elder Scipio, and mother-in-law of Scipio Aemilianus—

[1] *Frag. Poet. Rom.*, p. 131 (Baehrens) ; from the *Sota*.

[2] Quoted from the *Neoptolemus* by Cicero (*Tusc.* ii. 1) and Gellius (v. 15, 9).

[3] Cic. *Brut.* 79.

[4] *ibid.* 80 ; Plut. *Aem. Paul.* 6.

kept up the family tradition by providing her boys with the best Greek tutors of the day. She was rewarded by seeing her younger son, Caius Gracchus, acclaimed as the most brilliant orator of his generation.[1]

We have thus continuous evidence for the study of Greek rhetoric during the second century B.C.

The study of Greek philosophy is even better attested. Six years after the decree issued by the senate, three well-known philosophers came as ambassadors from Athens to Rome: Carneades, founder of the new Academy; Critolaus, head of the Peripatetic School; and Diogenes, a Stoic.[2] Following the example of Crates, they gave public lectures as well as their official address to the senate, and the enthusiasm which had been shown for Greek literature some years before was now renewed. Carneades, in particular, a master of dialectics and the most original mind in contemporary Greek philosophy, was especially admired. 'The young flocked to his lectures', Plutarch tells us, 'and the rumour went abroad that a magician had come to the city, capable of winning the youth of Rome away from all other pleasures in their enthusiasm for philosophy.' Cato was up in arms at once, and proposed that the senate should send the ambassadors about their business as soon as politeness would admit. And his opposition found support; for next year two Epicurean philosophers were convicted of teaching their doctrines to

[1] Cic. *Brut.* 104; 126; Plut. *C. Gracchus*, 19.

[2] Plut. *Cato maior*, 22; Gell. vi (vii). 14, 8.

the young, and were banished from the city.[1] But reactionary measures were in vain: Greek philosophy had come to stay. The younger Scipio's friendship with the Stoic philosopher, Panaetius, begins about this time, and is symbolic of the change in Roman ideals.[2] Even more significant is the attitude adopted by Cato in his old age. Never weary of denouncing the peril of too great familiarity with Greek ideas (' Greek literature will be the ruin of Rome ', he was fond of saying to his son),[3] he was bent upon keeping Latin literature free from contamination. ' Grasp your matter, and the words will come of themselves ', was the counsel which he opposed to all the lessons of Greek rhetoric:[4] and his famous definition of an orator as ' a good man able to speak ', was designedly opposed to Greek ideals.[5] Yet even he, in his old age, began to realize that, to make Rome independent of Greek literature, it was necessary to learn from the Greeks; and his last years were spent in a closer study of Greek literature.[6] There is something pathetic in this spectacle of the old man, who in his youth had brought Ennius to Rome, learning from his adversaries a trick he despised.

The facts just quoted show that the Hellenistic ideal of a culture based on the study of literature,

[1] Athen, xii, 547 A; Aelian, *Var. Hist.* 9, 12; Schanz, i. 1, p. 243.
[2] Schmekel, pp. 4 foll.
[3] Plut. *Cato maior*, 23; Pliny, *N. H.* xxix. 14.
[4] ' Rem tene, verba sequentur '; in *Rhet. Lat. Min.*, p. 374 (Halm).
[5] Sen. *Contr.* 1, *praef.* 9; Quint. xii. 1, 1.
[6] Cic. *de Sen.* 3; Plut. *Cato maior*, 2.

rhetoric, and philosophy was fully accepted in Rome by the middle of the second century B.C. A concrete example will illustrate the spirit in which Roman young men of the period entered upon the study of Greek literature and philosophy. Some years before the younger Scipio met Panaetius, he had come under the influence of another distinguished Greek, the historian Polybius. The origin of their friendship, as described by Polybius, is one of the most personal episodes in the history of Graeco-Roman education. Scipio Aemilianus came of a family that had been strongly influenced by the new Greek culture. His father, Aemilius Paulus, the conqueror of Macedonia, had done all that he could to provide his sons with the best Greek teachers of the day. Teachers of literature, rhetoric, and philosophy, teachers of sculpture and drawing, teachers of the art of hunting: all these had been brought over from Greece for the benefit of his boys.[1] Pydna was fought in 168 B.C., and Perseus, the Macedonian king, was captured by the Romans. Aemilius, as victor, had the right to dispose of his captive's property, and the royal library was set aside as his children's share in the booty.[2] Scipio's personal tastes bore witness to these early influences. After Pydna he spent his time in hunting through the royal park which had been let run wild during the four years of the war;[3] and throughout life his favourite author was

[1] Plut. *Aem. Paul.* 6; Cic. *de Rep.* i. 36.
[2] Plut. *Aem. Paul.* 28.
[3] Polyb. xxxi. 29, 3–6 (ed. Büttner-Wobst).

Xenophon—a natural taste for one who had been taught to hunt as well as to enjoy Greek literature.[1] But Polybius gives the truest insight into his character. The following passage refers to the year 167 B.C. or shortly afterwards, the year in which the Achaean hostages were first brought to Rome and then distributed among the different towns of Italy. Fabius and Scipio are the two sons of L. Aemilius Paulus; the former having been adopted by the grandson of Q. Fabius Maximus Cunctator, the latter by the son of P. Cornelius Scipio Africanus, the victor of Zama. The elder boy was at this time about twenty years old, the younger in his nineteenth year.

'The beginning of my companionship with the two boys was due to the loan of books, and to conversation on that subject. Our friendship soon became closer, and when the hostages were sent to the Italian cities, Fabius and Scipio begged their father to let me remain in Rome. This was granted, and our intimacy was already far advanced when the following incident occurred. One day, after we had left the house of Fabius together, Fabius turned down towards the forum, whilst Scipio went with me in another direction. After a little Publius said to me, blushing and in a low quiet tone: "Tell me, Polybius, why is it that, though there are two of us, you always address your conversation to my brother, putting him your questions, and giving him your replies, whilst you leave me alone? I suppose you share the opinion of my fellow-citizens. They all believe, so I am told, that I am too easy-going and lazy, the very opposite to a Roman in my way of life, because I do not care to plead in the courts. They say too (and this is what pains me most) that the family to which I belong needs a very different man at its head from what I am likely to be." I was puzzled at the boy's way of

[1] Cic. *Tusc.* ii. 62; *ad Q. fr.* i. 1, 23.

[2] To avoid obscurity, I have used the first person singular throughout.

opening the conversation (for he was then not more than eighteen years old), and answered: "Scipio, I beg of you, do not say such things; do not even think them. It was neither through contempt nor through any low opinion of your character that I acted as you describe; far from it. But your brother is the older, and that is why I always begin and end the conversation with him, addressing my answers and words of advice to him, and supposing that you share his opinion. But now I am glad to hear from you how pained you are at the idea of being less active than becomes one of your family. That shows your noble spirit, and I would gladly help you to say and do something worthy of your ancestors. You will have no lack of helpers, you and your brother, in the studies which are now, I see, absorbing most of your energies and ambitions: for I have noticed this tribe of teachers flocking over just now from Greece to Rome. But as for the problem which you tell me is now troubling you, I think you will find no one better suited than me to help you in your work." As I was still speaking, he caught my right hand in both his, and pressing it warmly, said: "Would that I could see the day when you would lay all other interests aside to live with me, and give me the whole of your attention! From that day I feel sure that I should soon prove worthy of my family and ancestors." I was overjoyed at the lad's eagerness to accept my proposal. But when I thought of the greatness of his family and the success of so many of its members, I began to hesitate. However, once that conversation had taken place, the boy was never out of my company, and seemed to care for nothing so much as his intimacy with me.'[1]

It would be a mistake to take this passage, with its curious undertone of Italian emotion, as typical of all Roman society of the period. Every Greek was not as loyal a friend as Polybius, nor was every Roman as eager for the glory of noble deeds as Scipio. Polybius himself goes on to contrast his young companion's idealism with the conduct of most young Roman noblemen of the period. All the vices

[1] Polyb. xxxi. 23, 4–24, 12 (ed. Büttner-Wobst).

of decadent Greek society had swept in on Rome, with the advent of the new culture; and Polybius quotes one of Cato's sayings, that to calculate the decline of public morality, one had only to compare the price of good-looking slaves on the market with the price of land or the price of a team of horses for ploughing.[1] But the important fact is, not that such inevitable abuses existed (they have always existed at the end of a great national effort), but that Roman idealism found its natural expression in Scipio's enthusiasm for Greek culture and Roman traditions. The spirit of companionship between Greek and Roman revealed in this friendship between Scipio and Polybius—a companionship which ignores the facts of military defeat and political inferiority—is indeed the keynote of the new culture. Cato's contempt for all things Greek seemed narrow and illiberal to Scipio and his friends, just as a mere slavish surrender to Greek intellectual superiority would have seemed to them unworthy of Roman dignity.

Nothing is more instructive in this connexion than the contempt which Polybius expresses for a contemporary Roman noble, A. Postumius Albinus, author of one of the Roman histories written in Greek, then a literary fashion.

'Aulus Postumius', he writes, 'merits our attention for a moment. Though born of a noble family, he was by nature a vain and idle babbler, eager to learn Greek customs and the Greek language, and devoting so much attention to these that he fell into extravagances, and by his conduct brought the whole of Greek culture into discredit in the eyes of older and more respect-

[1] Polyb. xxxi. 25, 5 (ed. Büttner-Wobst).

able Roman citizens. He even went so far as to write a poem and a history in Greek; and in his preface to the latter work he excused himself to his readers for being a Roman, and thus not having a full mastery of Greek idiom and Greek methods of composition. Cato's retort was much to the point: "I cannot understand the motive for such an apology. If the Amphictyonic council had ordered him to write his history, these excuses would perhaps have been necessary. But a man who takes it on himself to write a history under no compulsion, and then makes an apology for his blunders, is a thorough fool. He is as much a fool as though he had entered his name at the public games for the boxing-match or the *Pankration*, and then, when it was time for the match, came down into the *stadium*, pleading that he was unable to stand the fatigue and the blows. Such a man would very properly be laughed at and beaten for his pains, and these writers of history should get the same treatment for venturing to compete against properly trained men." Nor was this the only way in which Postumius imitated the worst features of Greek civilization. He was a lover of pleasure and a hater of work: as was proved by the event. For in the Phocian campaign, though the first to arrive in Greece, he pleaded ill-health and remained in Thebes to avoid the danger; but, the campaign once over, he was the first to send home an account of the victory, going into all the details as though he had fought the battles himself.'[1]

It is a Greek historian who is writing; yet Cato himself could hardly be more contemptuous.

[1] Polyb. xxxix. 1 (ed. Büttner-Wobst).

IV

THE NEW GRAECO-ROMAN CULTURE

'Quid P. Scipione, quid C. Laelio, quid L. Philo perfectius cogitari potest? qui, ne quid praetermitterent quod ad summam laudem clarorum virorum pertineret, ad domesticum maiorumque morem etiam hanc a Socrate adventitiam doctrinam adhibuerunt.' Cic. *de Rep.* iii. 5.

WHAT was the new Greek education which Aemilius Paulus was so eager to obtain for his sons, and which was henceforth dominant in the schools of Rome? Out of the turmoil created by the Sophistic movement of the fifth century B.C. two types of educational theory had been evolved: the scientific philosophy of Plato and Aristotle, and the rhetorical culture best expressed in the writings of Isocrates. The former of these two theories is familiar to all students of Greek philosophy. Its full development in the educational theory and practice of Aristotle is the type of a philosophical programme carried out in a rigorously scientific spirit. But the educational programme of Isocrates demands closer attention: partly for its intrinsic interest, partly because of its immense and abiding influence on Graeco-Roman education. For Isocrates was more than a successful teacher of rhetoric. In his writings on education he loves to call himself a 'philosopher',[1] and—in spite of Plato's irony—the claim is justified.

[1] Isocr. *Antid.* 50; 270; 285; Girard, p. 312.

For Isocrates was, quite genuinely, an educational idealist. In his theory, education is no mere preparation for lifelong scientific research: still less is it a method of learning absolute virtue or absolute truth. 'Let no man imagine', he writes in his first educational manifesto, 'that I hold justice can be taught. On the contrary I am convinced that there is no art capable of implanting justice and temperance in the hearts of those who are not naturally inclined to virtue. But I do believe that nothing helps so much towards the practice of virtue as the study of political wisdom and eloquence.'[1]

These words, which are re-echoed in his last public utterance,[2] made when Isocrates was eighty-two years old and had seen a brilliant company of orators and historians pass through his school, are characteristic of his whole teaching. Never a philosopher in the Platonic sense of the word nor a mere teacher of formal rhetoric, his aim was to train citizens for success in their own private life and in public affairs. Proudly conscious of this aim, he criticizes the rival theories of education proposed by contemporary teachers. For Plato's Academy and its elaborate scientific programme he has a half-tolerant contempt, somewhat embittered by a sense of injured personal vanity. 'There are some who have much skill in dialectics and who give all their time to astronomy, geometry and other such sciences. I do not think these men do harm to their pupils: on the contrary they do them good—less good than they themselves

[1] Isocr. *c. Soph.* 21. [2] Isocr. *Antid.* 274.

profess, but more good than most people think.' And he ends by recommending young men to spend some time at such studies, but not to give their whole lives to them; 'making shipwreck among the quibbles of the Sophists'.[1] For teachers of rhetoric who cared only for practical success in life (the allusion is to Tisias and Corax, and others who had written short manuals of the art of rhetoric) he has a scorn which recalls the fiery invective of Aristophanes, and which we shall meet again in Cicero's *de Oratore*. 'Teachers of hustling, grasping avarice', they would persuade the young that rhetoric is a mere trick which may be learnt like any alphabet.[2] For himself rhetoric is the noblest of all sciences, requiring from the student long effort and much sacrifice, but giving him in return knowledge and practical wisdom that are indispensable for civic virtue.[3] This opinion, expressed in language which is always eloquent, sometimes almost metaphysical in its phraseology,[4] lifts Isocrates high above other teachers of rhetoric, giving him an important place in the history of educational theory.

There is, of course, a radical contrast between the ideals of Plato and Aristotle, and the ideal expressed by Isocrates in these passages. It is the old contrast between the Sophists of the fifth century—Protagoras, Gorgias, Hippias, Prodicus, and the rest—on

[1] Isocr. *Antid.* 261–8; cf. *Busiris*, 23.
[2] Isocr. *c. Soph.* 9–13; *Antid.* 42.
[3] Isocr. *c. Soph.* 16–18; *Antid., passim*; *Panath.* 30–4.
[4] Cf. the use of ἰδέα in *c. Soph.* 16.

the one side and Socrates on the other; only now the contest, which had begun as a struggle for an ethical principle, has become in the main a rivalry between two intellectual theories. The story of that rivalry is familiar: Plato's rejection of rhetoric in the *Gorgias* and, to a lesser degree, in the *Phaedrus*; his expulsion of poets and artists from the ideal state in his *Republic*; the austere mathematical and metaphysical programme outlined in the seventh book of that dialogue, and carried into practice in his own teaching at the Academy; finally the more conciliatory attitude adopted by Aristotle, who admitted rhetoric as a formal science, akin to dialectics in its practical value, but less directly useful for philosophical inquiry.[1]

The stand thus made by Plato and Aristotle for the intrinsic value of metaphysical studies is of lasting importance in the history of ancient education. Modern terminology, which owes its present form to the classical definitions of Aristotle, distinguishes so sharply between philosopher and sophist that the confusion apparent in the thought of Isocrates seems inexcusable. But his contemporaries had a different perspective. Again and again in the literature of the fourth century B.C. the 'philosopher' or lover of wisdom (φιλόσοφος), whose mission is the study of truth for truth's sake, is confused with the 'sophist' or teacher of wisdom (σοφιστής), whose function is the work of practical education.[2]

[1] Ar. *Rhet.* i. 1; von Arnim, pp. 64 foll.
[2] von Arnim, pp. 11 foll.

Plato and Aristotle between them made the confusion finally impossible: henceforward 'philosopher' and 'sophist' are terms of clearly distinct meaning, and the study of metaphysical and ethical truth is recognized in every school of the Greek world as the highest form of human intellectual activity. But this newer and clearer terminology, directly due to the teaching of Plato and Aristotle, is also due in large measure, though indirectly, to the educational idealism of Isocrates. For the Isocratean programme expressed in the formula we have quoted, 'the study of political wisdom and eloquence' (τὴν τῶν λόγων τῶν πολιτικῶν ἐπιμέλειαν), had an immense influence on contemporary thought: to it is due the later Hellenistic notion of 'culture' or 'education' (παιδεία) as a necessary complement to free birth and intellectual attainments.

Plato and Aristotle themselves came under the influence of this teaching. In the *Laws*, his last attempt to win Athenian opinion for his social and political theories, Plato outlines a programme of educational studies very different from the earlier programme of the *Republic*. Metaphysics are no longer mentioned; and the study of mathematics is reduced to that elementary acquaintance with abstract reasoning which even Isocrates would have considered desirable.[1] This is a direct concession to public opinion, made by the most haughtily aristocratic of all Athenian philosophers: a concession, too, which must have been largely due to the success

[1] Plato, *Laws*, 817 E foll.; Wilamowitz, *Platon*, i, pp. 673 foll.

of the Isocratean programme. And the same policy of conciliating the educated, but unphilosophic, public is plain in the dual programme of studies adopted by Aristotle as a characteristic of Peripatetic teaching: in the morning private lectures, given to a class of select pupils; in the evening public lectures of a less technical character, given to all who cared to come.[1] There is the same dualism, too, in Aristotle's educational vocabulary. 'Philosophy' (φιλοσοφία) is reserved for the exclusively metaphysical side of his teaching, whilst 'culture' or 'education' (παιδεία) expresses the more popular section of his programme.[2] The words are not always kept clearly apart, for Aristotle's terminology is sometimes affected by the transition from one idea to another.[3] But the general distinction is proof that the ideal represented by Isocrates was acquiring a recognized, though subordinate, place in Greek educational theory.

A most curious illustration of this fact is the personification of Paideia as a new form of deity. In a familiar passage of the *de Corona* Demosthenes pours scorn on Aeschines for the clumsy apostrophe with which he had begun his peroration: 'O earth and sun and virtue and understanding and education (παιδεία), by which we learn to distinguish between what is becoming and what is unbecoming.'[4] Our school-texts simply re-echo the comments of Demos-

[1] Gell. xx. 5; Willmann, p. 50.
[2] Willmann, pp. 131 foll. [3] e.g. Ar. *Pol.* ii. 1263 b, 40.
[4] Aesch. *c. Ctes.* 260; Demosthenes, *de Cor.* 127.

thenes. But Aeschines was a shrewd pleader, and he probably was right in calculating that an Athenian jury would be flattered by an appeal to the latest intellectual catchword. The vase-paintings of this period reproduce the same allegorical personification —a sure proof of its popularity;[1] and it is worth nothing that four centuries later Lucian was to introduce Paideia as a deity into a famous scene, probably reminiscent of Aeschines and Demosthenes.[2]

No better type of this later Greek culture could be found than Polybius, the man whom destiny had marked out as the chief intellectual link between Greece and Rome. A scientist in the most rigorous sense of the word, an historian whose critical faculty has rarely been surpassed, a true patriot, and at the same time an enthusiastic admirer of Roman political greatness, he is the symbol of those intellectual and moral forces, still latent in Hellenistic Greece, which were to co-operate with Roman national tradition in forming the new Graeco-Roman culture. Polybius wrote no autobiography; but personal allusions abound in his history, and the story of his early education can be deduced from the character or quality of his work. He was evidently a man of wide reading, not merely in his own special science, but also in Greek poetry and prose. Homer and Euripides seem to have been his favourite poets; among prose writers the historians naturally occupy a foremost place, and in particular Timaeus, the object of

[1] Roscher, *Lexikon der Mythologie*, iii. 1, 1251.

[2] Lucian, *Somn.* 9, 14; *Pisc.* 16.

so many of his criticisms, Ephorus, Theopompus, and Callisthenes.[1] The study of rhetoric is also plain. Not that Polybius was a careful stylist; but only a student of rhetoric could have criticized Timaeus as he does for his use of rhetorical technique.[2] The influence of philosophy is even more plain: for Polybius is as much a political philosopher as an historian. And it is here that he is most typical of his age. If asked to define his philosophical position, Polybius would almost certainly have replied that he was a Stoic. Stoic influence is plain in all his work: most of all in the famous sixth book where he sums up the merits of the Roman state. His friendship with Scipio had brought him into personal contact with Panaetius, and the two thinkers had discussed together all the main problems of political theory.[3] But Polybius was far from being exclusive in his Stoicism. As might be expected from so scientific a mind, the influence of Aristotle on his thought is particularly strong;[4] and his admiration for Philopoemen, the Achaean national hero, who had studied philosophy under two pupils of Arcesilaus, made him an admirer of the Middle Academy.[5] Yet, for all his interest in philosophy, Polybius was no metaphysician and had little time for dialectical subtleties. Carneades, whose lectures had set all Rome talking, was too destructive in his scepticism

[1] Scala, pp. 63–86.

[2] Polyb. xii. 25 a, 5; 26, 9 (ed. Büttner-Wobst); Scala, p. 19.

[3] Cic. *de Rep.* i. 34; Scala, pp. 222 foll.

[4] Scala, pp. 126 foll.

[5] Polyb. x. 22, 2 (ed. Büttner-Wobst).

for the historian's practical sense, and Polybius holds him responsible for the Academy's decline.[1] Intellectual scepticism has never built an empire; and Polybius was an admirer of empire-builders.

This distrust of philosophy apart from practical experience is a link between Roman traditions and the culture of Hellenistic Greece: *philosophandum est, sed paucis; nam omnino haud placet.* With his usual instinct for dramatic truth, Cicero represents Scipio and Laelius as ever eager to recall Panaetius from metaphysics and physics back to the problems of ordinary life;[2] and Polybius would certainly have applauded their good sense. It was the same with his own favourite study. History, so he says in the preface to his great work, is only interesting as an object-lesson in political theory and moral conduct:[3] and Scipio, who made history instead of writing it, would have agreed.

The practical bent of both tutor and pupil is even more curiously evident in their attitude towards music and athletics. Scipio, with all his admiration for Greek traditions of culture, could never wholly reconcile himself to the manners of the *palaestra.* Cicero puts a diatribe against Greek athletics into his mouth in the *de Re publica*,[4] and Macrobius has preserved an interesting fragment on a similar topic from Scipio's speech against the *Lex Iudiciaria* of Tiberius Gracchus:[5]

[1] Polyb. xii. 26 c (ed. Büttner-Wobst).

[2] Cic. *de Rep.* i. 15; 19.

[3] Polyb. i. 1.

[4] Cic. *de Rep.* iv. 4.

[5] Macrob. *Sat.* iii. 14, 7.

'Our free-born boys and girls are going with lute and psaltery to the training-schools of professional actors. There they mingle with lewd companions, are taught unseemly antics, and learn to sing songs which our ancestors held dishonourable for all who were not slaves. When I was first told this, I could not believe that men of noble birth were giving their children such lessons. But I was taken to one of these dancing-schools; and there, by Heaven, I saw more than fifty boys and girls, among them one whose presence made me grieve for my country more than all the others: a senator's son, the son of a candidate for office, not less than twelve years old, with castanets, dancing a dance which no shameless slave-boy could dance without dishonour.'

In his eulogy of Scipio Polybius singles out this stern attitude towards the pleasures of decadent Greece as one of the finest traits in his hero's character.[1] And Polybius himself, though evidently familiar with all the customs and technicalities of Greek athletics,[2] was more of a Xenophon than a Plato in his preferences for out-door sport. Riding, hunting, the use of arms, all that concerns military and naval tactics: these are the topics on which he loves to dwell, and he tells us himself that a common interest in hunting was one of the main causes of his early friendship with Scipio.[3] There is only one exception to this community of tastes. In the fourth book of his *Histories*, Polybius tells the story of Cynaetha, a village in Arcadia. The village had won an evil name amongst its neighbours for brutal cruelty. Polybius, an Arcadian by birth, is anxious to clear his native land from a share in the discredit,

[1] Polyb. xxxi. 25, 8 (ed. Büttner-Wobst).
[2] Scala, p. 22, n. 1.
[3] Polyb. xxxi. 29, 8 (ed. Büttner-Wobst).

and explains that the people of Arcadia, knowing the rugged, barren nature of their country and fearing the moral effect of such surroundings, had given special attention to the development of dance and song in every village; they had even passed a law making musical exercises obligatory on every citizen of Arcadia until the age of thirty. The people of Cynaetha had failed to enforce this law: hence their inferior civilization with its traditions of brutality, which Polybius condemns.[1] The chapter is wholly characteristic of Greek, and especially Hellenistic, thought: recalling the newly discovered Hellenistic inscriptions, which provide for the endowment and upkeep of local schools of music, athletics and literature.[2] Polybius was a true Greek in his feeling for these refining influences; but neither Scipio nor Laelius could have written that chapter.

It is not easy to define the new Graeco-Roman culture which resulted from this fusion of Hellenistic civilization and Roman national traditions. Cicero, as usual, has the surest instinct; and he makes Scipio preface his view on the merits and demerits of the Roman state with these words:

'I give you my opinion, not as one wholly ignorant of Greek customs, nor as though I were anxious to see them preferred to our own; but as a Roman citizen who, thanks to his father's care, has received a good education and has been fond of study since boyhood; and who, none the less, owes more to experience and the lessons of home-life than to the study of books.'[3]

'Usu tamen et domesticis praeceptis multo magis

[1] Polyb iv. 20–1 (ed. Büttner-Wobst).

[2] Ziebarth, pp. 65 foll.; 123 foll.

[3] Cic. *de Rep.* i. 36.

eruditum quam litteris': the words might be taken as a motto for all Roman education of the republican period.

The new contact with Hellenistic culture added something which Cicero does not here express in words, though it underlies his whole philosophy. If the earlier traditions of Roman education are best summed up in the consecrated phrase *mos maiorum*, Cicero himself supplies elsewhere the term which best expresses the Graeco-Roman ideal of culture: not *mos maiorum* which stresses too heavily the value of family-tradition, nor παιδεία, which suggests systematic instruction in the art of civilization, but *humanitas*; a word which can be, and has often been, translated by such varying equivalents as 'culture', 'sympathy', 'courtesy', and 'human kindliness'. The word's significance can hardly be grasped without an analysis of Cicero's whole theory of education: its meaning was in doubt as early as the second century A.D.[1] When first the Romans began to use it as their equivalent for the Greek παιδεία, its derivation from *homo* made plain a fundamental difference of outlook. For the Greeks education was essentially an art, and παιδεία means 'education' as well as 'culture'. For the Romans education was something quite distinct from instruction in any art: *institutio* is their word for such instruction, whilst *educatio* expresses rather the result of home life and family traditions. So, too, *humanitas* brings into the Roman ideal of culture a note that is lacking

[1] Gell. xiii. 16.

in the more intellectual Greek ideal: the note of human dignity and human sympathy. Cicero himself uses the word mainly to express the intellectual and moral refinement of an educated man;[1] but the notion of human kindliness is never far absent from his thought. 'Homo sum; humani nil a me alienum puto': it is hardly an accidental coincidence that the famous phrase was first minted by a poet who was himself a member of the Scipionic circle. Its pregnant thought expresses much of that culture which Scipio and Laelius learnt from Polybius and Panaetius, and which Cicero in turn learnt from the last surviving members of the Scipionic circle.

[1] See the full analysis in Schneidewin, pp. 28–40.

V

UNDER MARIUS AND SULLA

'At vero ego hoc tempore omni noctes et dies in omnium doctrinarum meditatione versabar.' Cic. *Brut.* 308.

§ 1. *Plotius Gallus and the 'Latini rhetores'.*

It is a curious accident that the most disturbed period in Roman political history should be precisely the period during which we know most about Roman education under the Republic. But Cicero's lucky star sent him to school at a time when Marians and Sullans were busy killing each other in the streets of Rome: and the history of Roman education is very largely the history of Cicero's intellectual growth, maturity, and influence. During those years of turmoil and bloodshed Cicero was busy studying rhetoric and philosophy, and learning lessons that are more difficult to teach from men whose youth had been spent with Scipio and Laelius.

The Gracchi were the first to use the weapon of Greek rhetoric on behalf of the democratic cause. They had many successors and imitators: most notable of all, the two tribunes Sulpicius and Carbo. But the democratic spirit is apt to produce queer reactions in education. Roman democrats soon found Greek culture an expensive luxury, and they promptly denounced it as an idle folly of the rich. Marius himself was almost wholly uneducated. He had been brought up in Cicero's own town, Arpinum, and had gone straight into the army at an age when Cicero was only beginning his studies. 'He practised neither Greek eloquence nor the manners of town-life', says Sallust, who was a democrat in politics; 'and so his genius, being wholly devoted to an honourable profession, came rapidly to maturity.'[1] Plutarch tells the same story after his own fashion. 'It is said of him that he never learnt to read Greek, nor ever used the Greek language for any civilized purpose, thinking it foolish to learn a language which was taught by men who were themselves slaves'; and he adds that Marius might have had a happier end, if he had learnt to worship at the shrine of the Greek Muses and Graces.[2] Cicero, too, has a joke at the expense of one of the great demagogue's relatives: 'You care so little for all things Greek that you would not even take the Via Graeca to get home to your villa.'[3]

This studied opposition to Greek culture, and in particular to the study of Greek rhetoric, led to a curious episode in the history of Roman education. By way of preface to his *de Claris rhetoribus*, Suetonius inserts the text of two laws directed against the new schools of Greek rhetoric and philosophy. The earlier of the two is the *senatus consultum* of 161 B.C., banishing all teachers of philosophy and rhetoric from Rome.[4] The second must be quoted in full: it is an edict issued by the two censors of

[1] Sall. *Bell. Iug.* 63, 3; cf. 85, 32. [2] Plut. *Mar.* 2, 2.
[3] Cic. *ad Fam.* vii. 1, 3. [4] See above, p. 37.

92 B.C., Cn. Domitius Aenobarbus and L. Licinius Crassus.

'A report has been made to us that certain men have begun a new kind of teaching, and that young men are going regularly to their school; that they have taken the name of teachers of Latin rhetoric (*Latini rhetores*): and that our young men are wasting their whole days with them. Our ancestors ordained what lessons their children were to learn, and what schools they were to frequent. These new schools are contrary to our customs and ancestral traditions (*mos maiorum*), and we consider them undesirable and improper. Wherefore we have decided to publish, both to those who keep these schools and to those who are accustomed to go there, our judgement that we consider them undesirable.' [1]

The scholar who has done most to reconstruct the history of this edict considers the text as given by Suetonius a forgery: [2] his main argument being that the statement contained in the second sentence is inconsistent with Cicero's claim that Roman tradition was opposed 'to any detailed universal system of public education, obligatory by law'.[3] But the two statements are plainly not inconsistent: indeed they are rather complementary. And there is no sound reason for doubting the authenticity of a text which Suetonius had no conceivable motive for inventing. Moreover, the text itself is confirmed by two independent witnesses, both earlier than Suetonius. In the *de Oratore* Cicero makes Crassus defend his action in closing these new schools of Latin rhetoric:

[1] Suet. *Rhet.* 1; cf. Gell. xv. 11, where the term *Latini rhetores* is wrongly inserted in the decree of 161 B.C. This has led Wilkins (pp. 25 foll.) into error.

[2] Marx, p. 144.

[3] Cic. *de Rep.* iv. 3; above, p. 24.

the novelty of their name is insisted upon, as in the text of the edict.[1] And Tacitus gives a somewhat inaccurate version of the same story, confusing these *Latini rhetores* with teachers of rhetoric in general, in his *Dialogue on orators*.[2] Tacitus is plainly copying Cicero, whom he actually quotes, for most of his story ; but he has one accurate detail not to be found in Cicero's dramatized narrative. Probably for the sake of literary effect, Cicero makes Crassus the sole author of the edict. 'I abolished these new teachers by my edict', Crassus says in the dialogue ; and a little later : 'I thought it my duty as censor to put a stop to this danger.'[3] Suetonius, on the other hand, gives the edict as issued jointly by the two censors, Cn. Domitius Aenobarbus and L. Licinius Crassus : and his statement is confirmed by Tacitus.[4] Both men must have had some common, trustworthy source of information ; and the most probable source, to which both would have had easy access, was the authentic text of the edict itself.

Whether the text, as we have it, be genuine or not, the fact that Crassus and Domitius, acting conjointly, closed at least one school of Latin Rhetoric in 92 B.C. cannot be disputed : and the fact raises two or three curious questions. In the first place, the censorship of Crassus and Domitius is notorious in Roman history for constant quarrels between the

[1] Cic. *de Or.* iii. 93–5.
[2] Tac. *Dial.* 35.
[3] Cic. *loc. cit.* 93 ; 94.
[4] '[M.] Crasso et Domitio censoribus.' The M. is almost certainly a copyist's insertion ; see Gudeman *ad loc.*

two censors, which culminated in a famous *altercatio*.[1] What brought these two men together in 92 B.C., and on so curious an issue? Then again, the censor on whom Cicero throws the whole responsibility for the edict, L. Licinius Crassus, was the most distinguished orator of his day, and had done more than any man alive to apply the principles of Greek rhetoric to Roman oratory. Why should he close a school of Latin rhetoric? Lastly, who were these *Latini rhetores*, and what was their offence against Roman law or custom?

The last question may be answered first. Suetonius himself quotes from one of Cicero's letters to a certain M. Titinius, the statement that L. Plotius Gallus was the first to teach rhetoric in Latin at Rome;[2] and the elder Seneca and Quintilian both repeat Cicero's statement.[3] Now Plotius Gallus is known to us in another connexion: for Cicero refers to a poet, L. Plotius, an admirer and client of Marius, in his *pro Archia*,[4] and the identity of this poet with the teacher of Latin rhetoric is asserted by an early and well-informed scholiast.[5] This makes Plotius Gallus a democrat in politics, and fits in well with the only other item of information to be gleaned from our scanty sources. In 56 B.C., a year before Cicero published his *de Oratore*, Plotius was still alive as a very old man, and composed a speech for an unknown

[1] Pliny, *N. H.* xvii. 1–6; Cic. *de Or.* ii. 45; 230; Münzer in Pauly-Wissowa, v. 1326.
[2] Suet. *Rhet.* 2.
[3] Sen. *Contr.* ii, *praef.* 5; Quint. ii. 4, 42.
[4] Cic. *pro Arch.* 9, 20.
[5] Schol. Bob. *ad loc.*

Atratinus who had prosecuted Cicero's friend and correspondent, M. Coelius, for assault.[1] Coelius was a gay young aristocrat, and the name Atratinus has a plebeian ring about it. Probably Plotius Gallus was still loyal to his early political connexions.

At this point Cicero himself comes into the story. In the letter to Titinius which Suetonius quotes, Cicero gives us the following bit of autobiography.

> 'When I was a boy, I remember that a certain Plotius was the first to teach rhetoric in Latin. Everybody was crowding to his school: the keenest students of oratory were getting lessons from him, and I was disappointed at not being let go there myself. But I stayed away on the advice of friends who were very highly educated, and who held that practice in Greek declamation was a better training for talent.' [2]

The date must have been 93 or 92 B.C., when Cicero was just thirteen or fourteen years old: for the imaginary date of the *de Oratore* is 91 B.C., and Crassus there speaks of the whole episode as having taken place a year or two previously.[3] The distinguished friends who advised the young boy not to attend the classes of Plotius Gallus can have been no other than Crassus himself and his relatives, the two Scaevolae. For Cicero's father, though of obscure origin, had influential connexions in Rome. Either at Arpinum or Rome, he had sent his son to a school where he was a classmate of the younger Marius and Atticus;[4] and once the boy had taken the *toga virilis*—which would normally have happened in 93 or 92 B.C., for Cicero was born in 106 B.C.—

[1] Suet. *Rhet.* 2. [2] ibid. [3] Cic. *de Or.* iii. 93.
[4] Nep. *vit. Att.* 1, 4; cf. Cic. *de Leg.* i. 13; *Brut.* 307.

his father put him under the direct protection and patronage of Q. Mucius Scaevola the Augur.[1] Shortly afterwards, Scaevola died; and Cicero then transferred his allegiance to the Augur's relative and namesake, Q. Mucius Scaevola Pontifex. Licinius Crassus was son-in-law to Scaevola Augur, and the whole family was closely connected with the Scipionic tradition.[2] Cicero's fragment of autobiography thus appears in a new light when set in its social and political background.

That Plotius Gallus was forbidden to teach Latin rhetoric on political grounds, seems plain enough. Crassus and Domitius were personal enemies, but they were both aristocrats and conservative in politics. Nor can the plea that a school of Latin rhetoric was a novelty have been more than a pretence. Several other Romans were teaching rhetoric in or about this time;[3] and though we know nothing of the language in which they taught, it seems hardly credible that all their teaching was done in Greek. And M. Antonius, whom Cicero names as the great rival of Crassus in the Hellenized style of oratory, had written a Latin text-book of rhetoric before 91 B.C.[4] In the *de Oratore*, Cicero makes Crassus defend his action on the grounds given in the edict as preserved by Suetonius, with the added qualification that when competent Latin teachers could be found, they should be preferred to the

1 Cic. *de Am.* 1; *Brut.* 306.

2 Zielinski, p. 341.

3 Suet. *Gram.* 6; Cic. *Brut.* 102, 207; Schanz, i. 2, p. 452.

4 Cic. *de Or.* i. 94; *Or.* 18; *Brut.* 163.

Greeks. Nothing less could be expected in a dialogue written to present Greek theories of rhetoric in a Latin form. But this plea of incompetent teaching does not explain the drastic and almost unprecedented action of the censors. Their edict is only intelligible in the light of contemporary politics.

Were there other *Latini rhetores* besides Plotius Gallus? And did the movement survive the edict of 92 B.C.? No satisfactory answer can be given to the former question. All our authorities speak of teachers in the plural; but they are all influenced, directly or indirectly, by the language of the edict, and the censors had excellent motives for making a personal political manœuvre appear as impersonal as official language could make it. Plotius Gallus is the only *Latinus rhetor* whose name has come down to us, and there may well have been no other. And, since Plotius Gallus lived until well on into the fifties, his school of Latin rhetoric probably outlived the years of aristocratic supremacy in Rome. Varro mentions him as a well-known teacher of rhetoric;[1] and that is all we know of his personal history. But his school has left its mark in Latin literature.

Somewhere between the years 86 and 82 B.C.[2] an unknown student of rhetoric wrote in Latin for the benefit of his friend C. Herennius a text-book of rhetoric, closely modelled on the best Greek authors.

[1] Varro, *Sat.* 257 B (perhaps also 379 B; Marx, p. 148).

[2] Marx, p. 153; Warde Fowler in *Roman Essays*, pp. 96 foll., who gives good reasons for placing the date between 84 and 82 B.C.

The *ad Herennium*, as the book is now called (for its proper title is uncertain), is doubly interesting as being one of the oldest extant works in Latin prose, and a direct survival from the days of Marius and Sulla. Nothing is known of the author beyond the little that he tells us himself in the preface to his book. He was no longer a boy at school when he wrote, for he speaks of the pressure of family affairs; and he is old enough to prefer philosophy to rhetoric in his spare hours.[1] His friend Herennius was probably a democrat, for the *gens Herennia* was allied to the family of Marius;[2] and the anti-Hellenism of the democratic party is so deliberately emphasized by the anonymous author, that he may fairly be taken as a type of those who came under the influence of Plotius Gallus. In his preface to the first book, for example, he complains that Greek text-books are pedantic and unpractical; no Greek author is mentioned by name throughout the whole work; and the historical *exempla*, which are a regular feature of all such text-books, are deliberately taken from Roman, not Greek, history.[3]

This last point leads to a curious complication. From what we know of the *Latini rhetores* and their history, it seems certain that the anonymous friend of C. Herennius must have been himself one of the democratic party; and his Latin text-book has all the appearance of a literary manifesto. But it is not so easy to identify the author's politics from his

[1] *Ad Her.* i, *praef.* 1; iii. 40. [2] Plut. *Mar.* 5.
[3] *Ad Her.* iv, *praef.* 1; Marx, pp. 103 foll.

allusions to contemporary history: for many of his *exempla* are taken straight from the controversies of his own day. 'Should Scipio be exempted from the legal age for accepting office as consul?' 'Scipio Nasica is impeached before the tribunes of the people for the murder of Tiberius Gracchus.' 'Caepio is impeached before the tribunes of the people for the loss of his army.' 'Caepio is impeached for illegal action against Saturninus.' 'Should the Italians receive the rights of citizenship?' 'The murderer of Sulpicius is put on trial.'[1] These are all subjects on which any democrat would have been willing to declaim, and the excitement must have been intense if such subjects were actually debated in the classrooms of Plotius Gallus. But side by side with these revolutionary themes are others of the most orthodox conservatism. In one the slaughter of the optimates is reckoned a public disaster; in another the revival of public prosperity is due to the optimates; in two others Caepio's attack on Saturninus is praised as the action of a patriot.[2] These *exempla* were probably borrowed by the author from his own school-notes. Apparently Plotius Gallus allowed both sides a hearing in his school: perhaps he thought it safer to have both sides equally represented. In any case, there is plenty of material in the *ad Herennium* to justify Cicero's guardians in keeping him from such dangerous surroundings. It would never do for the conservatives to lose the

[1] *ad Her.* iii. 2; iv. 68; i. 21, 24, 25.

[2] *ibid.* iv. 12, 45; i. 21; ii. 17; Marx, p. 152.

gifted young student ; for stories o
cious talent were still told in the day

§ 2. *Cicero's Student-years*

Turned away from the school of Plo
Cicero did not lose his zeal for the study o
In the *Brutus* he tells the story of those early
days. Crassus was still a dominant person
the forum, and the other orators of the pe
Antonius, Sulpicius, Cotta, the young Hortensi
were at the height of their fame. 'I went to h
them all', he says, 'and was kept hard at wor
Every day I composed something myself, reading also and taking notes : for I was not content with the mere practice of declamation.'[2] Nor was rhetoric more than one of many enthusiasms. Cicero must have studied Greek literature at school, and Plutarch has a story that the orator's earliest dream was to become a great poet :[3] later he studied under the poet Archias.[4] More important was the influence of L. Aelius Stilo, Rome's first great scholar and the master of Cicero's contemporary, Varro.[5] From him Cicero learnt that love of his country's literature and history which remained a life-long possession : possibly also his remarkable familiarity with Ennius and the older Roman poets. Philosophy was first taught him by Phaedrus, an Epicurean ; but these early lessons made little impression. Phaedrus is mentioned affectionately in Cicero's correspondence,[6]

[1] Plut. *Cic.* 2. [2] *Brut.* 305. [3] Plut. *Cic.* 2.
[4] *pro Arch.* 1. [5] *Brut.* 207.
[6] *ad Fam.* xiii. 1, 2 ; *de Fin.* i. 16.

but his name is omitted in the two passages which give Cicero's intellectual autobiography.[1]

In the *de Oratore* Cicero claims that jurisprudence is the Roman counterpart to Greek philosophy;[2] his early friendship with the Scaevolae is thus of peculiar importance. By good fortune this friendship developed into a sort of private tuition. Scaevola Augur had the habit of bringing his young clients together when about to give a decision in his work as jurisconsult, and Cicero shared this privilege.[3] Like many another brilliant advocate, Cicero was no jurist; but these informal lessons in the house of Scaevola left their mark. Cicero never lost his respect for the greatness of Roman law, and for the people who had made that law. And his own acquaintance with the practical working of Roman law in the courts was always a valuable asset.

The *Brutus* tells how desolate Cicero found the years of Marian supremacy in Rome.[4] Books were his refuge from the constant pressure of public anxieties. And now for the first time he becomes aware of Greek philosophy. Phaedrus had been replaced by a Stoic tutor, Diodotus, who remained Cicero's companion until his death in 59 B.C.[5] But it was from another quarter that the decisive impulse came. Mithridates had just occupied Athens: the schools there had been broken up, and several Athenian philosophers were seeking refuge in Rome.

[1] *Brut.* 305 foll.; *de Nat. deor.* i. 6. [2] *de Or.* i. 195.
[3] *Brut.* 306; *de Am.* 1; *de Leg.* i. 13. [4] *Brut.* 305 foll.
[5] *Brut.* 309; *ad Att.* ii. 20, 6; *Tusc.* v. 113; *Acad.* ii. 115.

Prominent amongst them was Philo of Larissa, recently elected head of the Academy, and in every way a brilliant personality. Philo lectured on rhetoric as well as on philosophy,[1] and Cicero went to hear his lectures. 'I felt a wonderful enthusiasm for philosophy', he writes, 'and gave myself up entirely to Philo's teaching.'[2] A brief digression is needed to explain the character of this teaching, and the true reason of Cicero's enthusiasm.

Aristotle was the first Greek philosopher to teach rhetoric in his school, and his action pleased neither the disciples of Isocrates nor the disciples of Plato.[3] The controversy was continued during the next two centuries, and modern research has established the positions taken up by the four great schools.[4] Aristotle's practice was maintained by the later Peripatetics, and was also accepted by the Stoics, who held that the wise man can alone possess and impart all forms of knowledge. But the Stoics, unlike the Peripatetics, were interested only in the formal side of rhetorical theory, and Cicero complains that they neglected the practical work of developing the subject-matter (*inventio*) in favour of abstract definitions and sub-distinctions.[5] An exactly inverse relation existed between the schools of Plato and Epicurus, who agreed in their practice, but disagreed in theory. Plato had taught that rhetoric was

[1] *Tusc.* ii. 9, 26; *de Or.* iii. 110.
[2] *Brut.* 306; *Acad.* i. 13.
[3] Diog. Laert. v. 1, 3; Ar. *Rhet.* i. 1355a 21.
[4] See in general von Arnim, pp. 73 foll.
[5] *de Or.* ii. 157–9; *de Fin.* iv. 6; *Top.* 6.

harmful, and forbade it in his school. Epicurus admitted rhetoric as a true science, useful for political purposes ; but his system aimed at making men indifferent to all forms of political activity, and rhetoric was thereby excluded. The controversy gave rise to a whole literature of polemical essays. One of these essays written by an Epicurean named Philodemus was recovered during the last century, and it is from Philodemus that modern scholars have reconstructed this sequel to the controversy between Plato and Isocrates.

During the Hellenistic age Greek philosophy began to decline. Stoic teaching, with its pantheistic cosmopolitanism and its interest in scientific research, was best suited to the spirit of the age ; and its austere morality won the respect even of such Roman conservatives as Scipio and Aelius Stilo. In the growing indifference to metaphysical inquiry, all four schools began to conciliate public opinion by a more popular programme of studies ; and, by a strange irony of fate, Plato's school, with its memories of the *Gorgias* and the *Republic*, was the first to capitulate. Rhetoric was not at first formally admitted as a part of the curriculum taught in the Academy ; but, about the middle of the third century B.C., Arcesilaus, founder of what is known as the Middle Academy, introduced a new method of teaching philosophy. 'He was the first', says Diogenes Laertius, 'to debate both sides of a disputed question.'[1] Cicero gives a more detailed account : 'Arcesilaus intro-

[1] Diog. Laert. iv. 6, 28 ; von Arnim, p. 85.

duced the custom that his pupils should not ask him questions, but should themselves expose their own opinion. When they had spoken, he replied; and his pupils then defended their opinion as best they could. In other schools the pupils put their question and then remained silent: a practice which is now observed even in the Academy.'[1] It was, as Cicero notes, a reversion to the Socratic method; but it came at a time when scepticism had taken the place of Plato's metaphysical certitude, and its aim was to give dialectical skill rather than serious scientific knowledge.

Arcesilaus did not go without a successor: for the most famous teacher of the later Academy—and at the same time the most daringly sceptical of later Greek philosophers—was trained in the school under this new system. Carneades was, beyond question, an original and powerful thinker; but his fame was mainly due to the amazing brilliance of his dialectics, and his influence went far beyond the teaching of philosophy properly so called. Students of rhetoric flocked to hear his lectures, and to study his oratorical technique;[2] and it is characteristic that the lectures which he delivered in Rome during the embassy of 155 B.C. were remembered chiefly for their brilliant oratorical style.[3] The comparison with Hume's influence on modern philosophy is irresistible. Just as the Scotch philosopher's agreeably literary scepticism was a powerful factor in the thought of

[1] *de Fin.* ii. 2; *de Or.* iii. 80. [2] Diog. Laert. iv. 9, 62.
[3] Gell. vi (vii), 14, 8–10.

the eighteenth century, so Carneades exercised an abiding influence on the new Graeco-Roman culture which developed during his lifetime.

Philo of Larissa was a philosopher after the manner of Carneades: where possible, he pushed the new tendencies to their logical conclusion.[1] An open sceptic in his metaphysical teaching, he based whatever certitude he admitted on the testimony of moral conscience; and his action in teaching rhetoric as well as philosophy was a further break with the traditions of his school. Cicero, who had no metaphysical scruples, soon came under the spell of Philo's persuasive eloquence. Philo was indeed just the man to impress the young Roman student. Eager, quick-witted, impressionable, with a passion for study, Cicero was above all else a lover of the beauties of sound and language; and Philo was both an orator and a philosopher. New horizons began to open before the boy. Greek literature, Greek rhetoric, Greek philosophy; all these were seen to be necessary, if he was to achieve his youthful ideal and become the Roman Demosthenes. The brief narrative of the *Brutus* recalls those early days:

'During all this time [he is speaking of the years 86–83 B.C.] I spent my days and nights in the study of all forms of science. Diodotus the Stoic was my tutor, and he gave me lessons in other subjects, but above all in dialectics; these I learnt to know as a form of eloquence, closely-knit and compact. I was heart and soul at my work under this master, and his programme of study was wide and varied; yet I let no day pass without some practice in oratory. Every day I declaimed a piece with M. Piso or

[1] Zeller, iii. I, pp. 609 foll.; Susemihl, ii, pp. 279 foll.

Q. Pompeius or some other friend; often in Latin, but more often in Greek—partly because Greek, with its greater richness in rhetorical figures, is an excellent training for Latin oratory, partly because I could not hope to profit by the lessons and advice of the best Greek teachers unless I learnt to speak in Greek.'[1]

That last sentence reveals one of Cicero's day-dreams. No young student of his age and temperament could attend Philo's lectures in Rome, and not plan a tour through the schools of Greece and Asia Minor. For Athens was not the only centre of education in Hellenistic Greece, and Cicero was an eclectic by nature before ever he studied under Philo and Diodotus. But the Mithridatic war made all such plans impossible until Sulla's victorious return in 83 B.C.; and by that time Cicero, in needy circumstances and greedy of fame, was eager to start his career as a pleader in the forum. During the dictatorship of Sulla he made his first appearance in public, and for the next two years (81–79 B.C.) his name was gradually coming into prominence in the Roman law courts. But Cicero soon learnt that his delivery was faulty, and his friends urged that he must learn to speak in public without endangering his health.[2] The upshot was that in 79 B.C. he broke off his practice in the forum at the age of twenty-seven, and left Rome for his famous tour through Greece and Asia Minor. The details of that tour show how rich an inheritance Greek scholars were just then transmitting to the cultured classes of Roman society.

[1] *Brut.* 308–10. [2] *ibid.* 313.

From Rome Cicero went to Athens, where he spent six months. Here he studied philosophy in the lecture-halls of the Academy; but Philo was no longer there to welcome his former pupil. Antiochus of Ascalon, the new head of the school, had been Philo's great rival during the latter's lifetime, and, though an eclectic himself, was a declared opponent of Philo's scepticism.[1] His own system was largely influenced by Stoic thought, and Cicero, who speaks of Antiochus with great respect,[2] must have found his lectures congenial to his own temperament and early training. Antiochus, who made much of the Platonic tradition, taught only philosophy in his school, and Cicero had to go elsewhere for his lessons in rhetoric. At Athens he studied rhetoric under Demetrius of Syria; but the six months of his stay there were given mainly to philosophy. Then came a tour through the province of Asia, and Cicero gives the names of three or four professors of rhetoric whose lectures he attended.[3] But Rhodes was the culminating point in Cicero's experience. Here he met, though not for the first time, two men whose influence on his career as an orator and philosophic writer was only equalled by that of Crassus and Philo. Molo of Rhodes became Cicero's tutor in rhetoric, and helped more than any one else to correct the redundancies and looseness of Cicero's early style: a debt which Cicero never forgot.[4] And

[1] Zeller, iii. 1, pp. 618 foll.

[2] *Acad.* i. 13; ii. 113; *de Leg.* i. 54; *Brut.* 315.

[3] *ibid.* 315–16.

[4] *ibid.* 312, 316; Plut. *Cic.* 4.

it must have been at Rhodes, though Cicero omits this detail in his *Brutus*, that he studied under Posidonius, the famous Stoic philosopher and universalist, whom Cicero elsewhere names as one of the few men who did most for his education.[1] Posidonius, though nominally a Stoic and a disciple of Panaetius, was as eclectic in his theory as either Philo or Antiochus; and a brilliant literary stylist into the bargain. But it was his universal knowledge which most impressed his contemporaries; and it is no small claim for one man that he opened up new horizons of thought and learning for both Cicero and Julius Caesar.[2]

Cicero came back from his tour, as he himself puts it, 'not merely with added experience, but almost another man'.[3] His student years were over, and Roman literature was henceforth to be enriched by the full harvest of his maturity. But one permanent memorial of his student years still survives. In the preface to his *de Oratore* Cicero speaks of some 'school-boy notes which I published, rough and incomplete though they were, when I was still little more than a boy'.[4] These 'school-boy notes' are the *de Inventione*, which Cicero published when he was still a student of rhetoric, most probably between the years 85 and 80 B.C.[5] As a text-book of rhetoric the work is a failure. Cicero was not yet sufficiently master of his subject to do more than translate into

[1] *de Nat. deor.* i. 6; *de Fato*, 5; *Tusc.* ii. 61.
[2] See in general Zeller, iii. 1, p. 588; Susemihl, ii, p. 284.
[3] *Brut.* 316. [4] *de Or.* i. 5. [5] Schanz, i. 2, p. 467.

Latin the precepts of his Greek teachers, and his work suffers from comparison with the *ad Herennium* which seems to have been published about the same time. The author of the anonymous treatise, whoever he was, had a clearer brain than Cicero had yet developed, and his text-book, apart from questions of style, is in every way superior to Cicero's youthful effort. But the *de Inventione* is interesting as a promise of the future. Its preface, which Cicero seems to have borrowed from Posidonius,[1] deals with the time-honoured controversy between philosophy and rhetoric. Thirty years later Cicero published a dialogue which more than atones for the faults of his earlier essay, and states in eloquent language the solution to which his own experience and personal study had led him.

[1] Gerhäusser, p. 29; Philippson in Fleckeisen's *Jahrbuch*, vol. cxxxiii (1886), pp. 417 foll.

VI

THE 'DE ORATORE'

'Mea quidem sententia nemo poterit esse omni laude cumulatus orator, nisi erit omnium rerum magnarum atque artium scientiam consecutus.' Cic. *de Or.* i. 20.

§ 1. *Purpose of the 'de Oratore'*.

In a dedicatory letter to his brother Quintus, Cicero alleges as an excuse for publishing the *de Oratore* his anxiety to efface the memory of his youthful *de Inventione*.[1] The motive was natural enough: for Cicero was now at the height of his fame, and the earlier work was unworthy of his reputation as leader of the Roman forum. But there were other personal motives, to which he is careful not to allude. The *de Oratore* was published in 55 B.C., two years after his spectacular return from exile.[2] Cicero was at the height of his intellectual powers, and his ambition was as restless as ever. But politics were not going as the orator had hoped. His enemies were numerous and strong enough to keep his personal influence behind the barrier of their opposition; and the triumphs of his consulate were already remote. Ten years later Cicero found a refuge from similar troubles in the study of philosophy. Now he turns to the study of rhetoric and his old interest in the

[1] *de Or.* i. 5.

[2] *ad Att.* iv. 13, 2; *ad Fam.* i. 9, 23; Schanz, i. 2, p. 297.

problems of education. But the *de Oratore* is more than a manual of rhetoric or an essay on higher education. It is full of Cicero's political and intellectual idealism; and its dramatic background is deliberately chosen to emphasize the orator's connexion with the traditions of Scipionic Rome. Cicero was already planning the *de Republica* with its Scipionic reminiscences;[1] and the two dialogues were meant to convey, at a critical period in the orator's career, his mature views on Graeco-Roman literature, philosophy, and politics.

Less powerful, perhaps, as a stimulus to publication, but none the less important in the psychology of so human a character, were the domestic reasons which in 55 B.C. helped to renew Cicero's interest in the problem of education. Cicero's young son Marcus was at this time ten years old, his nephew Quintus a year older; and the orator had made himself responsible for the education of the two boys. There had been difficulties about a suitable tutor,[2] and in 54 B.C. Cicero talks of supplementing the tutor's classes with lessons of his own.[3] The *Partitiones oratoriae*, published in that year or a little later, are a sort of rhetorical catechism for the two boys, and show how practical the orator could be in his theory of education. The *de Oratore*, written a year earlier, shows the same preoccupation with the studies which young Marcus and Quintus were just

[1] *ad Q. fr.* ii. 12 (14), 1; iii. 5, 1; Schanz, i. 2, p. 342.
[2] *ad Att.* iv. 15, 10; vi. 1, 12; viii. 4, 1; *ad Q. fr.* iii. 1, 14.
[3] *ibid.* iii. 3, 4.

beginning. Cicero himself owed much to his father, and it is pleasant to think that the two boys were in his mind when he began work on the dialogue which was his favourite to the end.[1] Nor did his interest in the education of his son end with these classes in rhetoric. Ten years after the publication of the *de Oratore* he dedicated his *de Officiis* to Marcus, then a student of philosophy at Athens.[2]

Planned as an essay on the art of oratory, Cicero's dialogue is naturally more concerned with rhetoric than with any other subject. But the *de Oratore* is far more than a mere manual of rhetoric. With amazing literary skill Cicero has contrived to weave into the structure of his dialogue all that he had learnt from his early Roman patrons, from Diodotus, Philo, and Antiochus, and from the experience of thirty years in the forum. The result is a masterpiece which may not unfairly be called the orator's programme of educational reform: an appeal to the younger generation to imitate the example which he had set them, and to aim at a wider and nobler culture than was usual in contemporary Roman society. Later Cicero developed his programme in the *Brutus*, the *Orator*, and the lost *Hortensius*; but the *de Oratore* contains the substance of their doctrine, and is the fullest statement of Cicero's educational theory. Nor has any other of his dialogues had such permanent influence on the history of Graeco-Roman and European culture.

[1] *ad Att.* xiii. 19, 4.

[2] *de Off.* i. 1.

§ 2. *The 'artes liberales'*.

In his preface to the second book of the *de Oratore* Cicero sums up the education usually given in the Roman schools of his day under a convenient formula: *puerilis institutio*.[1] His own theory of education includes a supplementary course of higher studies, which he elsewhere terms *politior humanitas*.[2] The division is clear and logical, and it will be useful to analyse these two portions of his programme separately. But in practice there was no hard and fast division, for the recent break with tradition had thrown all Roman education into confusion.[3] Many of the orators whom Cicero criticizes in the *Brutus* had received no better education than the *puerilis institutio* as a preparation for public life. Others, like Cicero himself, had completed their studies in the intervals of work in the forum. It was only the few who passed regularly from one school to another, and completed their early education by higher studies similar to those which Cicero recommends.

The *de Oratore* has nothing to say about elementary schools; and the omission is characteristic. A Greek theorist would have detailed an elaborate scheme of education for the young, very much on the lines of Quintilian's programme in the *Institutio oratoria*. But Cicero was too much of a Roman to believe in such minutiae. In theory, at least, he would have agreed with Cato that the education of a child is primarily the parent's duty; and in the *Tusculan Disputations* the parent is named after the nurse and

[1] *de Or.* ii. 1; iii. 48, 125. [2] *ibid.* ii. 72. [3] *ibid.* i. 3.

before the schoolmaster in a list of those who influence children by their teaching and example.[1] The orator's own practice was somewhat different: force of circumstances was breaking up the old Roman tradition of home-life and parental education. Again and again in his private correspondence Cicero's love for his children reveals itself in some trifling incident.[2] 'The children are well', he writes to his brother in 54 B.C., 'they are busy at their lessons, are well taught and love us and one another.'[3] And again: 'Reading and study are my delight, and the quiet of my villa and, above all, the children.'[4] But Cicero never tried to teach his children as Cato taught his son. It was only when their study of rhetoric was well advanced that he thought of supplementing the teaching of Panaetius by some classes of his own: even then he was afraid that his more philosophic theory of rhetoric would be too much for the boys. 'Your boy likes declamation', he writes to his brother; 'I was that way myself once, and shall let him follow in my footsteps: I am sure that he will reach the same goal. But some day when I get him alone in the country I shall teach him my own theory and practice.'[5] It is all a pleasant reminder of the days of Cato and Aemilius Paulus; but the busy orator has only odd moments to spare for his interest in the two boys.

Cicero's real interest in education begins with the

[1] *Tusc.* iii. 2; *de Leg.* i. 47.
[2] See in general Schneidewin, pp. 185 foll.
[3] *ad Q. fr.* iii. 3, 1.
[4] *ibid.* iii. 9, 2.
[5] *ibid.* iii. 3, 4; cf. *ibid.* ii. 12 (14), 2; iii. 1, 7.

work usually done in the schools of literature and rhetoric; and here terminology is important. Roman usage distinguished clearly between the elementary schoolmaster (*ludi magister* or *litterator*, in Greek γραμματιστής), who gave lessons in reading and writing, and the teacher of literature (*grammaticus*, a term borrowed directly from the Greek γραμματικός) who taught prose-composition and poetry as well as grammar.[1] The Greek name shows that these teachers of literature and their schools were foreign to Roman tradition, and Suetonius dates the first schools of literature in Rome from the middle of the second century B.C.[2] But the *de Oratore* makes it plain that literature was only one of many subjects taught at Rome on the model of Greek school-programmes. In his preface to the first book Cicero enumerates the various *artes* taught in the schools of his day: philosophy, mathematics, music, literature, and rhetoric.[3] Elsewhere geometry and astronomy are expressly mentioned as part of the mathematical programme,[4] thus completing the seven *artes liberales* of the Middle Ages. Similar lists of the *artes* are to be found in contemporary Graeco-Roman literature. Varro included nine in his *Disciplinae*: grammar (or literature, for the term covers both subjects), dialectics, rhetoric, geometry, arithmetic, astronomy, music, medicine, architecture.[5] Vitruvius, writing for architects, gives literature, drawing, geometry,

[1] Suet. *Gram.* 4; Sandys, i, pp. 6–11; Girard, p. 224.
[2] Suet. *Gram.* 2.
[3] *de Or.* i. 8–12.
[4] *ibid.* i. 187; iii. 127.
[5] Schanz, i. 2, p. 438.

optics, arithmetic, history, philosophy, music, medicine, law, and astronomy—a strange medley![1] Seneca, who uses the term *artes liberales*, gives only literature, music, geometry, arithmetic, and astronomy; but he has his own reasons for omitting rhetoric and philosophy from the list.[2] And Galen, writing for doctors in the second century A.D., gives medicine, rhetoric, music, geometry, arithmetic, dialectics, astronomy, literature, and law.[3] Galen adds, as optional subjects, sculpture and drawing; but Seneca expressly excludes these two *artes* from his list.[4]

These lists, coming from such various sources, prove the existence of a regular curriculum of studies, not yet clearly defined in all its parts, but certainly including literature, rhetoric, dialectics, arithmetic, geometry, astronomy, and music. Seneca tells us that these subjects were called *artes liberales* in Latin, and ἐγκύκλιοι in Greek.[5] Cicero does not mention the Greek term, but frequently speaks of *artes liberales* or *liberalis disciplina*;[6] and once, in a characteristically Roman phrase, of *bonae artes*.[7] Vitruvius uses a curious phrase, half Greek, half Latin: *encyclios disciplina*;[8] and Quintilian gives the proper Greek form, which is also found in Strabo and Plutarch: ἐγκύκλιος παιδεία.[9]

The later history of these *artes liberales* is well

[1] Vitruv. i. 1, 3. [2] Sen. *Epp.* 88, 1–20; see below, p. 179.
[3] Galen, *Protr.* 14, 39. [4] Sen. *Epp.* 88, 18. [5] *ibid.* 23.
[6] *de Or.* i. 72; ii. 162; iii. 127. [7] *ibid.* i. 158.
[8] Vitruv. i. 1, 11; vi. *praef.* 4.
[9] Quint. i. 10, 1; Strabo, i, p. 13; Plut. *de Mus.* 1135 D; Ps.-Plut. *de Lib. ed.* 7 C; see also Colson's note on Quint. i. 10, 1.

known. Martianus Capella cast Varro's *Disciplinae* into allegorical form, and this curious text-book was the main source from which the Middle Ages derived their theory of *artes liberales*.[1] But the earlier history of the *artes* is more obscure, and takes us back once more to Aristotle. In classical Greek ἐγκύκλιος means 'ordinary' or 'of everyday occurrence' as well as 'cyclic'.[2] Aristotle frequently uses the word in this sense;[3] but once or twice we find the phrase τὰ ἐγκύκλια or τὰ ἐγκύκλια φιλοσοφήματα, where we should expect the more usual phrase τὰ ἐξωτερικά.[4] According to Gellius,[5] Aristotle's 'exoteric' programme of studies was designed for men of ordinary education, and included dialectics, rhetoric, and political theory: roughly speaking, the matter included by Aristotle in his *Organon*, *Rhetoric*, *Poetics*, *Politics*, and *Economics*. This programme differs considerably from the ἐγκύκλιος παιδεία described by Cicero, Varro, and later Roman writers; but the explanation is simple. Evidence for the work done in the schools of Hellenistic Greece is unusually abundant, and we know that a child's education was divided among a whole series of teachers.[6] First came the elementary schoolmaster

[1] Sandys, i, pp. 241 foll.

[2] See Stephanus, s.v., and (less fully) Liddell and Scott, s.v.

[3] Ar. *Pol.* i. 1255b 25; ii. 1263a 21; 1269b 35; cf. Isocr. 176 c.

[4] Ar. *Eth. Nic.* i. 1096a 3; *de Caelo*, i. 279a 30; Bonitz, *Index Aristotelicus*, p. 105a 27.

[5] Gell. xx. 5; Willmann, pp. 50 foll.

[6] See in general [Plato], *Axiochus*, 366 D–367 A; Girard, pp. 100 foll.; Walden, pp. 18 foll.

(γραμματιστής), who taught the child to read, write, and count, perhaps also to draw. Side by side with these lessons went classes in music, given by a special music-master (μουσικός), and gymnastic classes given by a professional teacher (παιδοτρίβης). Somewhat later, about the age of twelve, the boy went to a school of literature, where he was taught his Homer and poetry in general by the teacher of literature (κριτικός or γραμματικός); and at the same time he began the study of more advanced mathematics under a special mathematical master (γεομέτρης).

The connexion between these separate schools and the later ἐγκύκλιος παιδεία is plain. The latter programme of studies is simply a combination of the ordinary education given to Greek school-boys with the more elementary portion of Aristotle's 'exoteric' programme; and the Greek word ἐγκύκλιος accurately describes an education which was specially designed for the man in the street. When and where the various *artes* enumerated by Cicero, Varro, Vitruvius, and Seneca came to be recognized as parts of the εγκύκλιος παιδεία must remain uncertain; but the name or its equivalent (τὰ ἐγκύκλια μαθήματα) is common in Hellenistic literature. Diogenes Laertius, for example, tells us that the Cynics rejected τὰ ἐγκύκλια μαθήματα, and that Zeno considered the ἐγκύκλιος παιδεία useless: Chrysippus, on the other hand, said that τὰ ἐγκύκλια μαθήματα were very useful.[1] Similarly Athenaeus quotes two Hellenistic historians for the statement that Alexandria had educated both Greeks

[1] Diog. Laert. vi. 103; vii. 32, 129.

and 'barbarians' (this probably means the Romans) when the ἐγκύκλιος παιδεία was on the decline.[1] Seneca gives us the connecting link: for he tells us that Posidonius classified the arts under four heads. First place was given to the arts which teach virtue; second place to the arts 'which the Greeks call ἐγκύκλιοι and the Romans *liberales*'; third place to the 'frivolous' arts of dancing, singing, painting, and sculpture; and fourth place to all the arts that involve manual labour.[2] This classification proves that the 'encyclic' programme was well established by the end of the second century B.C., and throws a curious light on the classical use of the word 'art' (*ars* or τέχνη). As Cicero deals with the various *artes* throughout his *de Oratore*, one last digression must be pardoned by way of preface to his educational theory.

Modern education is so apt to measure knowledge by the mere accumulation of facts that we have ceased to regard the principle of specialization, even in schools, as anything abnormal. Greek principles of education were very different. Even in the most strictly scientific period of Hellenistic scholarship, specialization was unknown in the schools of Greece: knowledge, far from being an accumulation of facts, was essentially an art, first studied in its general principles and then applied in detail. Cicero's theory of scientific knowledge is borrowed directly from Greek sources: for him no true knowledge, whether of

[1] Athen. iv, p. 184 B.

[2] Sen. *Epp.* 88, 21–3; Gerhäusser, pp. 45 foll.

music, literature, rhetoric, or philosophy, is possible unless directed by the principles of an 'art'.[1] Each science has its own 'art', framed by human reason and binding together the details of knowledge in a single, coherent system; and the different 'arts' are themselves parts of a single, vast system of human knowledge which the philosophic mind can study in its first principles.[2] An example will make this concept more clear. Cicero complains that Roman law is not yet an 'art', because it lacks systematic form: he himself was in favour of reducing its endless details to a few general principles, easily learnt and easily applied.[3] So, too, ancient text-books of a particular science are usually called *artes* or τέχναι. Livy speaks of an *ars* for the guidance of priests in their sacrificial rites; [4] *ars grammatica* and *ars rhetorica* are both familiar terms; [5] and Cicero even compares the writings of Aristotle to a systematic *ars* of philosophy.[6] This use of the word τέχνη is a good example of the instinct for order and harmony which guided the Greeks in their intellectual activities as well as in their art. For the aim of the ἐγκύκλιος παιδεία was not to give every student a specialist's knowledge of detail (though detail abounds in the ancient text-books), but rather to put him in possession of such general principles as would later help him to a proper use of the knowledge

[1] *de Or.* i. 92; *Brut.* 152; *de Off.* ii. 6; Schneidewin, p. 309.
[2] *de Or.* i. 186–8; iii. 21; *de Nat. deor.* i. 9.
[3] *de Or.* i. 190; *de Leg.* ii. 47.
[4] Livy, xxv. 1, 12.
[5] *ad Her.* iv. 17; Quint. i, *Praef.* 23; 5, 54; ii. 17, 2; iii. 1, 1; Börner, pp. 12 foll.
[6] *Acad.* i. 17.

he had acquired. As Cicero puts it in his *de Oratore*: 'It is one thing to be a specialist (*artifex*) in any branch of science (*ars*); quite another to know enough for the ordinary purposes of life.'[1]

Cicero's *puerilis institutio* may be roughly identified with the Greek ἐγκύκλιος παιδεία with the exception of philosophy: he himself treats the term as synonymous with a 'liberal education'.[2] But Rome always modified what she borrowed, and the Roman *doctrina liberalis* has some significant omissions. Cicero himself remarks that his fellow-countrymen had little time for poetry and music, and confined mathematics to the practical work of counting and measurement.[3] Horace says the same of Roman mathematics;[4] and Cornelius Nepos, one of Cicero's personal friends and himself a most cultured man, tells us that music was always considered beneath the dignity of a Roman citizen, whilst dancing was looked on as a disgrace.[5] Here and there we find mention of Romans interested in mathematical theory; but they are noted as exceptions to the general rule.[6] And the name Fabius Pictor proves that a Roman with a taste for painting was an eccentric, who deserved special notice and even a special name.[7] Sulla liked music and could sing well—an oddity which is duly noted by Plutarch and

[1] *de Or.* i. 248; iii. 86.
[2] *ibid.* iii. 125.
[3] *Tusc.* i. 3–5.
[4] Hor. *Ars poet.* 323 foll.
[5] Corn. Nep. *Epam.* 1, 2; cf. Macrob. *Sat.* iii. 14, 7.
[6] *de Off.* i. 19; *Brut.* 175; *de Sen.* 49; *ad Att.* xiv. 12, 3.
[7] *Tusc.* i. 4; Pliny, *N.H.* xxxv. 19–23.

Macrobius;[1] but Cicero makes Crassus give the true Roman opinion of such arts in the *de Oratore.* 'He sings when asked', says Crassus of one of Scipio's friends, 'he is the father of a family and a Roman knight; but as a boy he learnt what is proper.'[2]

Latin school-terminology shows how little Roman and Greek interest in the *artes* coincided. For many of the subjects regularly taught in Roman schools, Greek names were retained to the end. *Grammatice, rhetorice, musice, mathesis, geometres, rhetor, philosophus*: these are all terms borrowed directly from the language of the ἐγκύκλιος παιδεία, and Quintilian holds that most of them had no proper Latin equivalent.[3] Suetonius, who was interested in the question and quotes Cornelius Nepos and Orbilius, holds that *litteratus* was at one time considered the correct Latin equivalent for γραμματικός,[4] and Quintilian gives *litteratura* as a translation of *grammatice.*[5] Cicero, who uses *rhetor* freely in his other works, is careful to use the term *magister dicendi* in his *De oratore,* and even apologizes for the occasional use of *rhetor.*[6] The scene of the *de Oratore* is laid in 91 B.C., when Cicero was a boy, and it would seem that the orator could remember a time when Roman purists objected to the use of all this Greek terminology. But at no time do we hear of a Latin equivalent for *musice, mathesis,*

1 Plut. *Sulla,* 2, 36; Macrob. *Sat.* iii. 14, 10.

2 *de Or.* iii. 87.

3 Quint. ii. 14, 1–4.

4 Suet. *Gram.* 4.

5 Quint. ii. 1, 4; 14, 3.

6 *de Or.* i. 84–7; iii. 92–4, 125.

and *geometria*: these were evidently considered too Greek to be Romanized. On the other hand, all the terms for elementary schools are purely Latin. *Ludi magister* is the ordinary word for an elementary schoolmaster, though Gellius and Apuleius both use *litterator*, the word given by Suetonius.[1] And the term *calculator* was invariably used for the teacher of elementary arithmetic.[2] This last word has a curious history. In the time of the Empire, it was accepted as a Greek word, at least in legal terminology. Modestinus, a Greek jurist of the third century A.D., uses καλκουλάτωρ in the Digest,[3] and the same barbarous form is found in the Greek version of Diocletian's Edict.[4] Horace was not so far wrong when he claimed simple addition and subtraction as a peculiarly Roman art.

§ 3. *The schools of literature and rhetoric.*

Apart from a superficial knowledge of music and mathematics, Roman education was given almost entirely in the schools of literature and rhetoric, and here Cicero's theory is of special importance. In the *de Oratore* Crassus defines the duties of a *grammaticus* as follows: 'to comment on the poets, to teach history, to explain the meaning of words, to impart a correct accent and delivery'.[5] These same duties are described by Quintilian in greater detail,[6] and

[1] Gell. xvi. 6, 1; xviii. 9, 2; Apul. *Flor.* 20.

[2] Mart. x. 62, 4; Isidor. *orig.* i. 3, 1; *Digest*, xxxviii. 1, 7, 5; *L.* 13, 1, 6; *Cod. Just.* x. 53 (52), 4.

[3] *Digest*, xxvii. 1, 15, 5.

[4] *Edict. Diocl.* 7, 67 (Mommsen).

[5] *de Or.* i. 187.

[6] Quint. i. 4, 2; 9, 1.

for the most part they require no comment. But two questions need to be discussed more fully. What authors were read in these schools of literature? And in what language were the lectures given?

Cicero makes neither point plain in his *de Oratore*; but the evidence of contemporary literature shows that Greek was still preponderant in the schools of Rome. Of the Latin *grammatici* mentioned by Suetonius many are not professional schoolmasters at all, but simply distinguished scholars who gave private lectures to their friends.[1] Orbilius and Valerius Cato are the only two professional teachers whose Latin origin is certain.[2] Another, M. Antonius Gnipho, was born in Gaul; but he knew Greek as perfectly as Latin, and was probably a native of one of the Greek-speaking towns in the Rhone valley.[3] All the other names mentioned by Suetonius as having flourished under the Republic are plainly Greek; and Cicero speaks of none but Greek tutors for his son.[4] Even more significant is the fact that when Cicero began to give his son and nephew classes in rhetoric, he preferred Greek to Latin as a medium for instruction.[5] Later on, he writes to his son at Athens and cautions him against neglecting his Latin exercises; [6] the caution shows which language was predominant in ordinary class-work. And all contemporary literature makes it plain that a knowledge of Greek was universal in the Roman society of

[1] Suet. *Gram.* 2, 3. [2] *ibid.* 9, 11. [3] *ibid.* 7.
[4] *ad Q. fr.* ii. 4, 2; iii. 3, 4; *ad Att.* iv. 15, 10.
[5] *Part. or.* 1–2. [6] *de Off.* i. 1; cf. *ad Fam.* xvi. 21, 5.

Cicero's day. Cicero's letters are full of Greek, and a whole section of his correspondence was actually written in Greek.[1] Roman orators were expected on occasion to deliver orations in Greek,[2] and Cicero's tutor, Molo of Rhodes, was allowed to address the senate in Greek without an interpreter.[3] Greek was the fashionable literary language, and more than one of Cicero's friends published works in Greek as well as in Latin.[4]

This preference for Greek as a literary language was not due to any lack of Roman patriotism. Cicero himself is never weary of repeating his admiration for Roman genius, and his conviction that Latin literature would eventually equal, perhaps even surpass, Greek literature.[5] But Greek, with its wealth of literature in prose and verse and its tradition of scientific criticism, was the inevitable language for use in schools. Orbilius, it is true, made his pupils learn their Livius Andronicus by heart,[6] and Cicero learnt his Twelve Tables as a boy ;[7] but what were Livius, Ennius, Accius, Plautus, Terence, and Lucilius when compared with Homer, Hesiod, the Attic tragedians, and Menander ? And the contrast was even more apparent in prose literature. Matters

1 Plut. *Cic.* 24 ; cf. Fr. Rühl in *Rhein. Mus.*, vol. lxx (1915), pp. 315–25.

2 Cic. *in Verr.* iv. 147 ; Quint. xi. 2, 50.

3 Plut. *Cic.* 4 ; Cic. *Brut.* 312.

4 *ad Att.* i. 19, 10 ; Plut. *Lucull.* 1 ; cf. R. Daebritz in *Philologus*, vol. xxiv (1911), pp. 267–73.

5 *de Or.* i. 13–15 ; iii. 95 ; *Or.* 22–3 ; *Tusc.* i. 1–6.

6 Hor. *Epp.* ii. 1, 69.

7 *de Leg.* ii. 59.

were different fifty years later when a classical Latin literature had been created by Cicero himself and the writers of the Augustan age. But all the enthusiasm and energy of Orbilius could not make early Latin literature attractive to schoolboys, and it has been well said that Horace's satire on Ennius, Naevius, and the rest expresses 'his parting shot at the criticisms he had been made to swallow in his boyhood'.[1] For good or for ill, Cicero's words are true: 'We Romans have gone to school in Greece; we read their poets and learn them by heart, and then we think ourselves scholars and men of culture.'[2]

In addition to the study of literature and grammar, Cicero assigns to the *grammaticus* the task of giving his pupils 'a correct accent and delivery'.[3] The phrase refers primarily to lessons in reading aloud and declamation; but Cicero may also have had in mind some elementary lessons in rhetoric. For in the early days of Graeco-Roman education rhetoric was taught by the professor of literature, and the custom was still occasionally observed in Rome as late as the first century A.D.[4] Even when the two professions had been separated by custom, it was quite a common practice for the *grammaticus* to end his course of literature with an informal introduction to the study of rhetoric.[5] Cicero himself regularly speaks of *grammatici* and *rhetores* as distinct professions; but the division between their schools was not so clearly

[1] Nettleship, *Essays* (Second Series), p. 52.

[2] *Tusc.* ii. 27.

[3] *de Or.* i. 187.

[4] Suet. *Gram.* 4.

[5] Quint. ii. 1, 3–6.

marked as modern authors are apt to assume.[1] No exact age can be fixed for the change from one school to another. Cicero himself thought of going to hear Plotius Gallus when he was only thirteen or fourteen years old,[2] and he got a tutor in rhetoric for his son when the boy was only eleven.[3]

These facts speak for themselves, and the *de Oratore* makes it quite plain that Cicero regarded rhetoric as part of the *puerilis institutio*.[4] Indeed Cicero's main purpose in writing the dialogue was to persuade his contemporaries that the instruction usually given in the schools of rhetoric was inadequate as a preparation for true oratory. Crassus is here the spokesman of Cicero's own experience.

> 'Thanks to my father's care', he says, 'I was well educated as a boy; but I cannot say that I was taught everything that I am now telling you should be taught in our schools. For I began my career as an advocate at an unusually early age, and was only twenty-one years old when I arraigned one of our foremost citizens and orators. The forum was thus my class-room, and my teacher was none other than the customs, laws, institutions and traditions of the Roman people.' [5]

And he adds that once his school-days were over, he had no time for study save in the intervals of public business.[6] Antonius, who serves as a foil to Crassus in the dialogue, insists even more strongly on the difficulty of adding anything to the school-curriculum. 'Before we have time to begin our studies', he says, 'we are caught in the stream of ambition

[1] Jullien, p. 340; Wilkins, p. 77; Blümner, p. 332.
[2] Suet. *Rhet.* 2; see above, p. 64.
[3] *ad Q. fr.* ii. 4, 2.
[4] *de Or.* i. 163, 244; ii. 100; iii. 38.
[5] *ibid.* iii. 74–5.
[6] *ibid.* iii. 85.

and public life.'[1] Cicero himself might have re-echoed those words, were it not for a lucky break-down in his health; many of his contemporaries must have been less fortunate.

According to Cicero, the existing schools of rhetoric did more harm than good. The classes were given by some Greek professor who had never been to the forum in his life, and who taught oratory by rule of thumb.[2] At best, he could teach you to deny the charge brought against you in the court, or, if that trick failed, to accuse your adversary of some mis-demeanour; as a last resort he might help you to justify your conduct by one or other of his stock excuses.[3] The irony is severe; but Cicero's own *de Inventione* and the parallel treatise *ad Herennium* are there to prove how far Greek rhetoric had gone on the path of formal and barren scholasticism. Both works are based mainly on a famous text-book, now lost: the *Rhetoric* of Hermagoras. Quintilian names the author of this text-book as an outstanding figure in the history of rhetoric,[4] and his influence on later Greek and Roman writers can hardly be overesti-mated. A brief account of his theory will illustrate the type of teaching which Cicero is criticizing in the *de Oratore*.

Hermagoras flourished about the middle of the second century B.C.[5] Stoic influence was at the time predominant in Greek thought, and Hermagoras

[1] *ibid.* i. 94; ii. 1–4.
[2] *ibid.* ii. 75; Laurand, pp. 5 foll.
[3] *ibid.* iii. 70, 75.
[4] Quint. iii. 1, 16.
[5] Thiele, p. 177; Susemihl, ii, p. 472, n. 83.

must have studied under some teacher of that school. Stoic terminology is a marked feature of all his theory, and the Stoic habit of division and subdivision was applied by him in all its logical completeness to the study of rhetoric. Cicero's complaint that Stoic theory neglected the practical aspects of oratory in favour of abstract definitions and subdistinctions [1] is doubly true of Hermagoras. Aristotle had based his theory of rhetoric on a careful induction of what had been found useful in the practical work of oratory. Hermagoras deduces his theory from an abstract definition of the subject-matter (*ζήτημα*); [2] calculates with almost mathematical accuracy the exact place for each portion of the speech; can tell you where to put in a digression, and where to make an emotional appeal; and has little or nothing to say about the various types of oratorical style.[3]

The natural consequence of this theory was a change in the value set upon different kinds of oratory. Aristotle had divided oratory into three general types: speeches in favour of or against a future action (*συμβουλευτικόν*), speeches in favour of or against a past action (*δικανικόν*), and speeches composed as a display of oratorical power (*ἐπιδεικτικόν*).[4] Epideictic oratory is assigned the lowest place, and Aristotle's preferences are for the first of the three types, with its greater opportunities for

[1] *de Or.* ii. 159; *Top.* 6.
[2] Thiele, pp. 33 foll.
[3] *ibid.*, pp. 84 foll., 140 foll.
[4] Ar. *Rhet.* i. 3; Volkmann, pp. 16 foll.

true political oratory. Hermagoras inverts this order. Epideictic oratory is still assigned the lowest place, but legal arguments are preferred to more general political or philosophic themes.[1] In Cicero's language, all his rules are about *causae* (or *controversiae*, as they were called in the Augustan age): little or nothing is said about abstract *quaestiones* (*suasoriae*).[2] And the reason is obvious. Hermagoras and his school had a passion for the ingenious logical development of an argument, and these qualities were shown to better advantage in the statement of a complicated case than in the discussion of some great issue. Hermagoras himself carried this ingenuity to strange extremes: he was prepared to write a speech on a murder-case, developed according to the best rules of his school, but without a single allusion to the crime or the victim.[3]

Yet with all its faults, Greek scholastic rhetoric was a wonderfully elaborate and logical science, and Cicero himself admits that he could not improve on Greek rhetorical technique.[4] Indeed, the orator never seems to be quite at home when he is writing about the technical details of rhetorical composition: the *τεχνολογία* of his dialogue, as he calls it in one of his letters.[5] It is only in the third book of his *de Oratore* that this *τεχνολογία* becomes alive: for there, as in

[1] Thiele, p. 78.

[2] *de Or.* iii. 78; for the terminology Sen. *Contr.* i, *praef.* 12; below, p. 164.

[3] Thiele, p. 64.

[4] *de Or.* i. 23, 145; Laurand, pp. 12 foll.

[5] *ad Att.* iv. 16, 3.

the *Orator*, he is writing on the theory of literary style, and Cicero well knew that he was the greatest living master of the art—possibly the greatest that has ever lived. Yet, strange to say, the Greek technicalities which he so disliked did more than his literary style to save his essays on rhetoric from the fate of so much else that he wrote. A modern scholar[1] has calculated that we have lost in all nearly fifty of Cicero's speeches, whole collections of his correspondence, and such famous dialogues as the *Hortensius*, the *de Gloria*, and, with the exception of a few fragments, the *de Re publica*. But the essays on rhetoric have been preserved in their entirety: not merely the *de Oratore*, the *Orator*, and the *Brutus*, but the youthful *de Inventione* and such minor works as the *Topica*, the *Partitiones oratoriae*, and the *de Optimo genere oratorum*. And of them all none was more read and commented than the 'school-boy notes' for which Cicero felt it necessary to apologize:[2] precisely because they reflected more faithfully than any other of his treatises the despised τεχνολογία of the Greeks. Literature has her ironies as well as life.

§ 4. *History, Law, and Philosophy.*

'The lesson of my dialogue', says Cicero in the *de Oratore*, 'is that no man has ever become a great orator unless he has combined a training in rhetoric with all other branches of knowledge';[3] and again, even more clearly: 'In my opinion no one can hope

[1] Zielinski, p. 131. [2] Schanz, i. 2, p. 402; Zielinski, p. 321.
[3] *de Or.* ii. 5.

to be an orator in the true sense of the word unless he has acquired knowledge of all the sciences and all the great problems of life.'[1] Rhetoric is only a subordinate part of this universal programme, and Cicero expressly approves the attitude of Crassus in his dialogue, who 'neither wholly devoted himself to the study of rhetoric as do those who measure all eloquence by its art, nor wholly rejected it, as so many philosophers have done'.[2] Cicero himself remained a student of rhetoric all his life. As late as 66 B.C., when he held the office of praetor, he was still a pupil of M. Antonius Gnipho;[3] and twenty-three years later he gave private classes in rhetoric to the two consuls of the year, Hirtius and Pansa.[4] Rhetoric belongs thus to the *politior humanitas* as well as to the *puerilis institutio*: but of all the higher studies recommended in the *de Oratore* it is the least important.

Since Cicero claims the whole field of knowledge for his ideal orator, no precise definition of his educational theory is possible. In the early chapters of his dialogue he argues that, since an orator must be ready to speak with knowledge and persuasive power on every subject, he must be familiar with rhetoric, ethics, psychology, history, jurisprudence, military and naval science, medicine and physical sciences such as geography and astronomy.[5] The catalogue is interrupted by a laugh from one of the bystanders, and Cicero plainly feels the need of an

[1] *ibid.* i. 20, 72. [2] *ibid.* i. 110. [3] Suet. *Gram.* 7; *Rhet.* 1.
[4] Suet. *Rhet.* 1. [5] *de Or.* i. 45–73.

apology: Hellenistic ideas of universal culture look well on paper, but the line must be drawn somewhere in practical life. And so, with a plea for the busy Roman who has to govern the world as well as write speeches, he announces his intention of dealing only with the subjects which are of practical importance for judicial and deliberative oratory.[1] The course of the dialogue makes it plain that these subjects are principally three in number: history, jurisprudence, and philosophy. But the argument assumes throughout the dialogue that the future orator has already received the 'liberal education' of an ordinary Roman school-boy. 'Were I to train an orator', says Antonius in the second book, 'I should begin by finding out the extent of his powers. He would need to have studied literature for a while, to have been to some school and done some reading, and been taught the rules of rhetoric.'[2] That is an excellent colloquial definition of the *puerilis institutio*.

Cicero was not the first Roman to emphasize the educational value of history, and in particular of national history. Cato, who 'wrote out a history with his own hand and in large characters' for his son's use, spent the last years of his life writing a history of Rome:[3] and the Roman Republic never lacked historians. Yet history was never taught as a separate subject in the Roman schools. This curious anomaly is explained by the methods of

[1] *de Or.* i. 21.
[2] *ibid.* ii. 85.
[3] Plut. *Cato maior*, 20; Corn. Nep. *Cato*, 3, 3.

Graeco-Roman literary education. Prose-authors were not usually read in the schools of literature, and whatever general instruction was given took the form of oral commentary on the poets read in class. That is why Cicero names the teaching of history as work done by the *grammaticus*,[1] and Quintilian takes the same practice for granted more than a century later.[2] In Greece, where national legend and history were the sole theme of epic and drama, the practice was natural enough: even the dullest of teachers could hardly fail to teach history well with Homer and Aeschylus as his text-books. But in Roman schools under the Republic, where Greek literature was usually preferred to Latin, the study of national history was bound to suffer. The only early Latin poem certainly read at school was the Latin *Odyssey* of Livius Andronicus.[3] More national poems were to hand, if the teacher cared to use them: the *Punic War* of Naevius, the *Annals* of Ennius, and the *Satires* of Lucilius. Orbilius, so Horace's language implies, made his pupils learn them all by heart,[4] and Cicero's numerous quotations show that he had read them with an eye to Roman history. But Orbilius is a lonely figure in the history of Roman education, and Cicero was noted for his antiquarian interests. The average Roman boy probably left school with a singularly vague knowledge of his country's past: and the standard of knowledge drops notably under the Empire. Graeco-Roman

[1] *de Or.* i. 187.
[2] Quint. i. 8, 18; below, p. 198.
[3] Hor. *Epp.* ii. 1, 69.
[4] *ibid.* ii. 1, 60, 85.

mythology takes the place of national history in ordinary class-work at school, and the change accounts in part for the general dullness of later Latin literature.

But the schools of literature were not wholly to blame for this neglect of history. What was lacking in their curriculum might very well have been supplied by the teachers of rhetoric, and Plotius Gallus proved that interest in national history, even in contemporary politics, could be stimulated by the selection of good subjects for declamation. Here again the Greeks had given the lead. Many of the declamations commonly in use as school exercises dealt with incidents of Greek history, notably those described by the great classical historians. The overthrow of the tyrants, the Persian wars, Cleon, Pericles and Alcibiades, Aeschines and Demosthenes, Alexander the Great: these were the favourite topics and personages, and it was obviously easy to combine such exercises with an intelligent study of Greek history.[1] But Roman teachers found it easier to borrow than to imitate, and the preference for Greek subjects becomes more marked as time goes on. Cicero's *de Inventione*, written at a time when the influence of Plotius Gallus was still strong, shows both tendencies at work. Many of his *exempla* are borrowed directly from Greek legend and history: Epaminondas and Alexander appear in company with Ajax, Clytemnestra, and Orestes.[2] But the

[1] Kohl, pp. 8–89.

[2] *de Inv.* i. 11, 18, 31, 55, 69, 93.

number of Roman subjects is even larger. The legend of the three Horatii, the Samnite and Punic wars, the war with Philip of Macedon, the destruction of Carthage and Corinth, two incidents from the Cimbric wars, the revolt of Fregellae, and a minor campaign conducted by Cicero's own patron, L. Licinius Crassus, in 94 B.C.: these are typical *exempla* from his early work,[1] and the same principle of selection is applied in the *Partitiones oratoriae*, written in 54 or 53 B.C.[2] Unfortunately Cicero's example was not followed by later teachers of rhetoric: the tradition of the *Latini rhetores* ends with Plotius Gallus.

Cicero's own interest in the study of history, and his theory of historical criticism, illustrate both the merits and defects of Graeco-Roman education. 'To be ignorant of what happened before you were born', he writes in the *Orator*, 'is to live the life of a child for ever. For what is man's life, unless woven into the life of our ancestors by the memory of past deeds?'[3] And his praise of history in the *de Oratore* has become a commonplace: 'witness of the ages, light of truth, life of tradition, teacher of life, messenger of antiquity', so runs his litany of praise.[4] But history has a double value in his eyes: it links us with the past, and it is invaluable as a store-house of rhetorical illustrations. 'An orator must know all the countless lessons of antiquity', he says in the *De oratore*;[5] and in the *Orator*, the *Brutus*, and the

[1] *ibid.* i. 11, 17; ii. 52, 72, 78, 91, 111, 124, 171.
[2] *Part. or.* 104–6. [3] *Or.* 120. [4] *de Or.* ii. 36.
[5] *ibid.* i. 18, 201.

Hortensius he stresses the value of national history for the same purpose.[1]

Cicero has often been criticized for this pragmatic view of history, and has been made responsible for the rhetorical sins of later Roman historians.[2] A sentence from the *Brutus* is sometimes quoted as proof conclusive of the charge. Cicero has just quoted the death of Coriolanus as an example of national ingratitude, and then hesitates because Atticus is present, and he is not sure of his facts. 'No matter', says Atticus; 'and in any case there is no objection to falsifying history in rhetoric, for the sake of a neat point.'[3] The words are spoken half jestingly in the dialogue; but Cicero's critics have not always been noted for their sense of humour and the orator's least words, even those spoken in a dramatic dialogue, must be brought in judgement against him. Yet Cicero's theory of historical criticism is not far to seek. 'The first rule of history', he tells us in the *de Oratore*, 'is to say nothing wilfully false; the second, wilfully to suppress no truth'; and on these foundations he builds a theory of scientific criticism which would do credit to any modern University professor. An accurate knowledge of chronology and geography, due attention to the causes which underlie superficial phenomena, the laws of human psychology, the standards of public morality and the moral influence of great personalities: all these

[1] *Or.* 120; *Brut.* 322; *Hortens.* fr. 26 (Müller).

[2] Peter, i, pp. 12 foll.; Norden, pp. 81 foll.; Schanz, i. 2, p. 388.

[3] *Brut.* 42.

Cicero requires, and his concluding precept is a warning against too much attention to literary ornament.[1]

Yet it is just this passage which has most irritated modern critics: for it begins with the assertion that history 'is in great measure the function of an orator'.[2] And in the preface to his *de Legibus*, where he distinguishes history from poetry, he goes on to say that history 'is the most oratorical of all forms of composition'.[3] These are startling definitions at first sight, and seem to cancel the value of Cicero's more scientific theory. But 'oratory', in Cicero's language, means artistic prose, not rhetoric; and the great orator's theory of criticism makes nonsense only when this distinction is forgotten. His comparison between history and oratory merely expresses the common judgement of antiquity, that historical composition is an art and must be guided by an artist's standards. Greek critics, perhaps with a surer instinct, preferred to compare history with poetry as a creative art, and Quintilian sums up their theory in a well-known phrase: 'History is akin to poetry, and may be called a poem in prose.'[4] Cicero himself more than once speaks of oratory as almost a form of poetry,[5] and there is perhaps no fundamental difference between his definition and Quintilian's.

Cicero's theory of historical composition is best illustrated by the criticisms of earlier Roman

[1] *de Or.* ii. 62–4. [2] *ibid.* ii. 62. [3] *de Leg.* i. 5.
[4] Quint. x. 1, 31. [5] *de Or.* i. 70; iii. 27; *Or.* 66.

historians with which he has prefaced his *de Legibus*. Even Cato is too jejune for his taste, and Coelius Antipater too clumsy. 'We have no historian in Latin literature', is his final verdict; and he ends with a hint that he himself might yet live to write the classical history of Rome.[1] More than one of his contemporaries shared this hope, and Cornelius Nepos mourned Cicero's death as the loss of a great historian.[2] But the orator's ideal historian came a generation later. Livy's stately preface, with its claim that Roman history is 'greater than the history of any other State, more venerable and richer in examples of human virtue',[3] exactly expresses Cicero's thought: and Livy's sober judgement, breadth of historical perspective, and highly-trained literary sense are durable proof that history can be nearly allied to oratory and yet remain true to its proper functions. After all, how many modern historians are as well worth reading as Livy?

Cicero's interest in Roman jurisprudence is very closely connected with his interest in Roman history. In the *de Oratore* this connexion is expressly stated, and is linked with the names of Cicero's early patrons, L. Aelius Stilo and Q. Mucius Scaevola;[4] in the *de Legibus*, which begins with a digression on Roman history, Scaevola is named as the man to whom Cicero mainly owed his interest in Roman law.[5] National pride is the inspiring motive of this double interest.

[1] *de Leg.* i. 5–8. [2] Corn. Nep., fr. 26 (Halm); Plut. *Cic.* 41.
[3] Livy, *praef.* 11. [4] *de Or.* i. 193. [5] *de Leg.* i. 13.

'Let the philosophers rage as they will', says Crassus in the *de Oratore*; 'I give my opinion in spite of them. When due attention is paid to the origins and principles of our laws, a single copy of the Twelve Tables has greater weight and authority than the libraries of all the philosophers in the world. If all men take pride in their country, as is their first duty, what must be our love and enthusiasm for a country which is the sole home of valour, empire, and true nobility? We are all children of our country. That is reason enough for being familiar with its genius, its traditions, its civilization; but we may also feel sure that our ancestors were as wise in the framing of their laws as in the winning of this vast Empire with all its resources.'

And he goes on to compare the Twelve Tables with the constitutions of Lycurgus, Draco, and Solon; bidding his readers rejoice in the contrast between Roman law and the 'confused and almost laughable' attempts of other nations.[1]

Can an orator be also a jurist? The question is important for Cicero's educational theory, but no very satisfactory answer can be found in the *de Oratore*. Two speeches of the dialogue deal with this problem: one by Crassus, who favours an extensive study of Roman public and private law, the other by Antonius, who maintains that oratory and jurisprudence are separate sciences, each demanding the study of a lifetime.[2] No formal solution is given to the problem, but the whole structure of the *de Oratore* shows that Cicero's sympathies were with the idealism of Crassus. Antonius appears consistently in the dialogue as the type of a successful advocate who owes his success entirely to natural talent: he affects a contempt for Greek culture, and boasts

[1] *de Or.* i. 195–7.

[2] *ibid.* i. 166–203, 234–55.

openly that he has never made a serious study of Roman law.[1] Crassus, on the other hand, is represented as an accomplished lawyer, under the influence of his father-in-law, Scaevola Augur.[2] The name at once suggests Cicero's own experience, and there is more than one hint in the *de Oratore* that Crassus is an idealized portrait of Cicero himself.[3] Ten years later, in the *Brutus*, Cicero elaborated the comparison in detail, comparing himself with Crassus and his friend Servius Sulpicius with Scaevola Pontifex:[4] a double comparison which must have been in Cicero's mind when writing the earlier dialogue, for he there makes Crassus narrate an anecdote of himself and Scaevola exactly parallel to his own handling of Sulpicius in the *pro Murena*.[5]

But Crassus is not allowed to have it all his own way in the argument about legal studies, and it is a fair conclusion that Cicero himself admitted a compromise as possible. In his speech on the subject Crassus pours scorn on the Greek custom of hiring legal advisers (πραγματικοί) to do the research-work necessary for a sound legal opinion.[6] Antonius takes him up on this point in his reply, and has no difficulty in showing that the Roman practice of consulting eminent jurists was based on the same principle, differing only in the greater honour accorded to professional lawyers by Roman tradition.[7] Cicero

[1] *de Or.* ii. 1–4; i. 172, 248.
[2] *ibid.* i. 40, 234; *Brut.* 145.
[3] Cf. for example *de Or.* i. 255 with *de Leg.* i. 11.
[4] *Brut.* 150.
[5] *de Or.* i. 242–3; *Brut.* 194–7; *pro Mur.* 23–9.
[6] *ibid.* i. 198.
[7] *ibid.* i. 250–3.

is plainly aware of the inevitable distinction between a good advocate and a good lawyer, and the contemporary history of Roman law shows that Antonius is voicing a common experience of the Roman forum. Cato, according to Cicero, was a great jurist as well as a great statesman and orator;[1] and Cicero's second patron, Scaevola Pontifex, was still able to combine the two functions of jurist and advocate.[2] Crassus belonged to the same traditions, and Cicero calls him 'the best lawyer of our orators', whilst Scaevola was 'the most eloquent of our lawyers'.[3] But Scaevola Augur, the most famous jurist of the family, was no orator;[4] and the break between the two professions is best illustrated by a story which has found its way into the Digest. Servius Sulpicius, the greatest jurist of Cicero's day, began life as an orator. Like most of his contemporaries, he depended on others for his knowledge of the law, and had once to consult Scaevola Pontifex on a difficult legal problem. Scaevola gave his solution, which Sulpicius could not understand. A second question provoked the retort that it was a shame for a Roman advocate to be so ignorant of Roman law. Sulpicius took the rebuke to heart and gave himself wholly to the study of law:[5] as Cicero puts it, 'he preferred to be first in the second of Roman sciences rather than second in the first'.[6] Henceforward, no Roman was famous

[1] *de Or.* i. 171; iii. 135.
[2] *ibid.* i. 180.
[3] *Brut.* 145–8.
[4] *de Or.* i. 39, 214.
[5] Pomponius in *Dig.* i. 2, 2, 43.
[6] *Brut.* 151.

as both orator and jurist, and the distinction between the two professions becomes more and more marked with the ever-increasing complexity of Roman civil and criminal law.

§ 5. *Cicero's theory of the 'doctus orator'*.

Cicero's plea that the true orator must also be a great jurist needs to be qualified in the light of his personal experience: and the same is true of his argument that great oratory is impossible without a study of philosophy. That argument is the culminating point of his educational theory, and is stated by Crassus in the third book of the *de Oratore*.[1] Early in the dialogue Crassus had already stated the argument in brief outline, and had stressed in particular the need for a careful study of psychology, ethics, and politics: physics and even dialectics could safely be neglected as less directly useful for an orator.[2] Antonius makes a similar claim in the second book, once more stressing ethics and politics as essential for the work of public oratory.[3] And now in the third book Crassus re-states the case for philosophy with all the eloquence at his command.

The pith of the argument as stated by Crassus in his great speech may be summed up in a single phrase. Cato had given a famous counsel of perfection to his son: 'Grasp your matter, and the words will come of themselves.' [4] Cicero's advice is founded on the same principle, but its wording illustrates all

[1] *de Or.* iii. 52–143. [2] *ibid.* i. 53–7. [3] *ibid.* ii. 65–70.
[4] Cato, *apud* Jul. Vict. in *Rhet. Lat. Min.*, p. 374 (Halm).

the difference between his theory of eloquence and Cato's more primitive standards. 'Abundance of matter will give abundance of words':[1] that principle is at the root of all his educational theory, both in the *de Oratore* and in the later dialogues. Psychology, ethics, politics, dialectics, even physics: all these must be studied, not for their own worth, but because without them an orator may often fail in the knowledge required for his practical work. 'The choice of words, their proper place, and rhythm is easily learnt, or can be picked up without any teaching. But the matter of oratory presents a vast field, which the Greeks have neglected and have thereby been the cause of making our young men ignorant even in their knowledge.'[2] Crassus maintains that the proper function of philosophy is to remedy this defect in an orator's training; and the 'wise men' whom he chooses as his ideal types of culture are not Plato, Aristotle, and Chrysippus, but (strange assortment!) Themistocles, Pericles, Theramenes, Gorgias, Thrasymachus, and Isocrates.[3]

This list of Greek names suggests that Cicero, according to his usual practice, is borrowing from some Greek source; and a little later in the dialogue Crassus actually uses a Greek term (πολιτικοί φιλόσοφοι) to describe these 'philosophic statesmen', for we can hardly call them philosophers.[4] From what Greek source is Cicero borrowing? The question is of peculiar interest, because this speech of Crassus

[1] *de Or.* iii. 125. [2] *ibid.* iii. 93. [3] *ibid.* iii. 59.
[4] *ibid.* iii. 109.

marks the culminating point of the *de Oratore* and of Cicero's whole educational theory. Two German scholars have attempted an answer, and the result of their research appears to be solidly established.[1] The whole trend of Cicero's thought in the *de Oratore*, his insistence on the ideal of a cultured orator (*doctus orator*) [2] who shall combine the excellences of both orator and philosopher, suggests at once the influence of the New Academy as it had been recreated by Arcesilaus and Carneades. In the *Orator*, Cicero makes the famous confession that his eloquence was due to 'the groves of the Academy, not to those workshops, the schools of rhetoric'; [3] and in his *de Fato* he stresses the kinship between his ideal of oratory and the teaching of the Academy.[4] These confessions give point to a passage in the *de Oratore* where Cotta, one of the minor personages in the dialogue, breaks the silence which has followed the great speech of Crassus with the remark: 'I do not know what influence you have had on the others, but you have won me heart and soul for the Academy.' [5]

Can we go farther, and locate more precisely the Greek philosopher whom Cicero is following? Cicero had studied under two heads of the New Academy, Philo and Antiochus, and it is tempting to claim one or other as the real author of the theories which Cicero attributes to Crassus. But the evidence is not conclusive for either philosopher. One passage in

[1] von Arnim, pp. 102 foll.; Kroll in *Rhein. Mus.*, vol. lviii (1903), pp. 552 foll.

[2] *de Or.* iii. 143; Kroll, *loc. cit.*

[3] *Or.* 12.

[4] *de Fato.* 3.

[5] *de Or.* iii. 145.

which emphasis is laid on the distinction between Old and New Academy—a distinction denied by Philo—suggests the hand of Antiochus.[1] But a single phrase is not sufficient to decide the question, for Cicero uses his Greek sources very freely; and the general trend of the argument suggests rather Philo's influence. Philo, we know, taught rhetoric as well as philosophy: a practice commended by Crassus in the *de Oratore*.[2] And the praise of Carneades,[3] followed by an open criticism of Plato's attitude towards oratory,[4] can hardly be reconciled with the loyalty professed by Antiochus for the Old Academy. Lastly, it should be noted that the very ideas which Crassus states so fully in the *de Oratore* are to be found, stated more briefly but no less clearly, in Cicero's youthful *de Inventione*:[5] a work written and published when his enthusiasm for Philo's lectures on rhetoric and philosophy was still a recent experience.

Wherever Cicero got his theory of the *doctus orator*, he believed in it heart and soul. Ten years later he wrote the *Orator* and the *Brutus* in defence of the same ideal;[6] but neither dialogue contains a passage of greater eloquence than this speech of Crassus in the third book of the *de Oratore*. Its concluding words must be quoted in full:

'Some may prefer to call the kind of philosopher who can

[1] *de Or.* iii. 67; *Acad.* i. 13; Kroll, *loc. cit.*, p. 555.
[2] *de Or.* iii. 72, 80, 110.
[3] *ibid.* iii. 68–71.
[4] *ibid.* iii. 60, 122, 129.
[5] *de Inv.* ii. 6–8.
[6] *Or.* 14; *Brut.* 322.

supply us with material for our eloquence an orator; others may prefer to call the orator whom I have defined as uniting wisdom with eloquence a philosopher. To me the name matters little, provided it be granted that praise is due neither to the man who knows his matter but cannot give it expression for lack of the ability to speak, nor to the man who is never at a loss for words but has no information to give. Certainly, were I forced to choose, I would prefer to be wise and unable to speak than to be a talkative fool; but when I am asked what is the highest excellence of all, I give the palm to the cultured orator (*doctus orator*). Grant me that such a man is also a philosopher, and the controversy is at an end. But if the distinction be maintained, then, since the perfect orator has all the philosopher's learning, whilst knowledge of philosophy does not always imply eloquence, our adversaries must admit a certain inferiority. They reject our eloquence, of course; but it seems to me beyond dispute that oratory is capable of adding a certain perfection to their science.' [1]

A detail of method to which Crassus refers in this speech is interesting in the light of Cicero's own practice. Ever since the days of Hermagoras, who had divided the subject-matter of declamation into topics of an abstract nature or 'theses' (θέσεις), and topics of a more personal character (ὑποθέσεις),[2] the former class of topics had formed a sort of disputed territory between the schools of rhetoric and the schools of philosophy. Cicero gives us examples of these 'theses' in his *de Inventione*: 'Is there any good save upright conduct?' 'Are the senses true or false?' 'What is the shape of the world and the size of the sun?' [3] Hermagoras had claimed for the schools of rhetoric the right to teach such abstract subjects: and his claim had been resented by the philosophers as an infringement of their traditional

[1] *de Or.* iii. 142–3. [2] Thiele, pp. 27 foll. [3] *de Inv.* i. 8.

rights.[1] In his *de Inventione* Cicero rejects the claim of Hermagoras as pretentious. 'He understands neither the meaning of his own words nor the full extent of his claim'; and he adds that he would sooner take away from Hermagoras the right to teach rhetoric than grant him the right to teach philosophy.[2]

Yet in the *de Oratore* Crassus expressly includes the practice of declaiming such abstract 'theses' in his programme of higher studies. 'At present', he says, 'it is in use only among the Peripatetics and in the Academy, but the ancients, from whom we borrow all our theory of oratory and all our eloquence, used it regularly'; and he specially commends Philo for his revival of the old practice.[3] There is here no real change from Cicero's earlier teaching in the *de Inventione*. Hermagoras is there condemned, not because his abstract 'theses' are a bad training for the future orator, but expressly because of his own lack of culture and general education. In the *de Oratore* Crassus assumes that 'theses' will be practised under the guidance of a philosopher like Philo, or at least of one who has studied philosophy. Cicero is plainly thinking of his own practice. In a letter written to his brother only a year after the publication of the *de Oratore* he compares his method of teaching with the methods of his nephew's tutor, Paeonius; and the epithet with which he qualifies his own method (θετικώτερον) is reminiscent of this

[1] Plut. *Pomp.* 42; Arnim, pp. 93 foll. [2] *de Inv.* i. 8.
[3] *de Or.* iii. 107–8, 110.

controversy.[1] It is amusing to note that Cicero's nephew found his uncle's lessons dull, and preferred the tutor's livelier classes. The orator consoles himself with the thought that he himself had passed through the same stage, and that the young boy will one day be as good a philosopher as his uncle. In the meantime practice in these semi-philosophical theses would be useful as a link between the study of rhetoric and the study of philosophy; and that is precisely the purpose they serve in Cicero's whole educational theory. Cicero drives home this lesson, not only in the *de Oratore*, but also in the *Brutus*, the *Topica*, and the *Tusculan Disputations*.[2]

6. *Ciceronian* '*Humanitas*'.

Literature, rhetoric, history, law, philosophy: these are the five studies without which Cicero's ideal of the *doctus orator* would be incomplete. Later in life, under the stress of public calamities, Cicero tended to lay greater emphasis on philosophy as the sole moral and intellectual guide for men; and the *Hortensius*, in which Cicero himself takes the place held by Crassus in the *de Oratore*, whilst Hortensius plays the part of Antonius, was written to convey this lesson. But the contrast between Cicero and Hortensius is not the contrast suggested to our modern thought by the words 'philosopher' and 'orator': it is rather the contrast between an orator who lacks Cicero's *politior humanitas* and a man—call

[1] *ad Q. fr.* iii. 3, 4.

[2] *Brut.* 322; *Top.* 79–86; *Tusc.* i. 7; ii. 9.

him *doctus orator* or πολιτικὸς φιλόσοφος, as you will—whose culture is due to the studies commended by Crassus in the *de Oratore.* The few fragments of the *Hortensius* which have survived show us this fundamental unity of Cicero's teaching. Here, as in the *de Oratore,* Cicero presupposes the *artes liberales* as the basis of a philosophic culture ;[1] and the dialogue, which was written to praise philosophy at the expense of oratory, contained a panegyric of oratory by Hortensius[2] and of history by Lucullus.[3]

The truth is that neither 'philosopher' nor 'orator' is an adequate term for Cicero's ideal. Only one word gives full expression to that ideal—*humanitas,* or its corresponding epithet, *humanus* : a word which recurs almost on every page of the *de Oratore.*[4] In the short conversation between Crassus and Scaevola which serves as prologue to the whole dialogue, the word's full meaning is illustrated by a characteristic phrase. Crassus has delivered a panegyric on oratory, and his praises culminate in the double claim that oratory carries to its highest perfection the faculty of speech by which man is distinguished from the brute creation, and has also raised man from the debased surroundings of primitive society to the cultured social civilization with which his listeners are familiar (*ad hunc humanum cultum civilemque*).[5] The word, here used for the first time in the dialogue, runs like a thread of gold

[1] *Hortens.* fr. 23 (Mueller). [2] *ibid.* fr. 45 (Mueller).
[3] *ibid.* fr. 11 (Mueller).
[4] Schneidewin (pp. 31–40) gives a full lexicography.
[5] *de Or.* i. 33.

through all the discussions and digressions of the *de Oratore*, taking on countless shades of meaning under the play of Cicero's thought, but always recalling in its varying use the fundamental idea of human excellence which Crassus here expresses. To be a man in all that is most human, and to be human in one's relations with all other men ; that is Cicero's ethical and social ideal, and his educational theory is based on the same principle. A phrase from a later portion of the *de Oratore* shows why this ideal inevitably led Cicero to formulate a programme of studies which is as Greek as it is Roman. 'We must borrow our virtues from Rome and our culture from Greece' : [1] those few words express in brief form the whole of Cicero's educational theory.

But the word *humanitas* has a double interest for readers of the *de Oratore*. Several modern critics have failed to find unity of thought or dramatic construction in the great orator's favourite dialogue: [2] a failure which arises from their wrong interpretation of Cicero's purpose in composing the dialogue. Some have interpreted the *de Oratore* as an attack on the *Latini rhetores* : [3] others as an attack on Greek teachers of rhetoric ; [4] others as a criticism of all forms of rhetoric as taught in Greek and Roman schools.[5] This last view comes nearest to the truth, but is incomplete as an interpretation of the dialogue

[1] *de Or.* iii. 137. [2] Schanz, i. 2, p. 298.
[3] Marx, p. 141 ; Norden, i, p. 222.
[4] Laurand, p. 11, n. 1, gives names.
[5] *ibid.* pp. 1–12 ; Kroll in Teuffel (ed. 6), i, p. 394.

as a whole. Cicero's object is positive, not negative: he has an ideal of his own to put forward, and that ideal is best expressed by the word *humanus*. Once this central thought is grasped, the dramatic unity of the dialogue becomes apparent. The three books of which it is composed represent three distinct conversations held in the course of two days. During the first conversation Crassus is represented as the ideal type of *humanitas*, illustrating the dual meaning of that elusive word as much by the courtesy of his manner as by the intellectual refinement of his talk: his *humanitas* in this double aspect is especially noted by Cotta, the imaginary reporter of the conversations.[1] Antonius, on the other hand, appears as a foil to Crassus in all this part of the dialogue. He boasts openly of his lack of education, and is never weary of insisting on the practical needs of life.[2]

Next morning all is changed. Antonius opens his discourse on rhetoric with a praise of oratory almost identical in its phraseology with the earlier speech of Crassus;[3] and his theory of rhetoric is in perfect harmony with the principles expounded by Crassus in the first and third books. Since Antonius is here the principal exponent of Cicero's theory, the change of front could hardly have been avoided; but Cicero is too good an artist to let it pass unnoticed. In an admirably vivid preface to the second book he explains that Antonius affected in public a contempt for all literary studies which he did not really feel;[4]

[1] *de Or.* i. 27.
[2] *ibid.* i. 80–95, 208, 260–4.
[3] *ibid.* ii. 33–8 = i. 30–4.
[4] *ibid.* ii. 1–4.

and a further explanation is inserted in the dialogue itself. Crassus, who has been listening to the opening speech of Antonius, interrupts him with a gesture of surprise: 'You have been civilized over-night, Antonius, and are now a man' (*Nox te nobis, Antoni, expolivit hominemque reddidit*); and he goes on to contrast his new attitude with the lack of culture (*humanitas*) which he had shown on the preceding day.[1] Cicero could hardly have given a plainer hint as to the inner meaning of his dialogue. It is true that Crassus is represented throughout as an admirer of all Greek studies, whilst Antonius is more concerned with the practical problem of success in the forum; and there is no formal reconciliation of the two views at the end of the dialogue. But both men are united in their opinion that culture—*humanitas*—is essential to all great oratory and to all proper civic virtue. Both would have agreed with the words which Cicero puts into the mouth of Scipio in that other dialogue which he planned as the companion-piece to his *de Oratore*: 'We are all called men, but only those of us are men who have been civilized by the studies proper to culture' (*Appellari ceteros homines, esse solos eos qui essent politi propriis humanitatis artibus*).[2] All the teaching of the *de Oratore* is contained in that phrase.

[1] *de Or.* ii. 40.

[2] *de Rep.* i. 28.

VII

REACTION AND ITS CAUSES

'Cogitaret plebem, quae toga enitesceret: sublatis studiorum pretiis, etiam studia peritura.' Tac. *Ann.* xi. 7.

1. *Decline of the Roman Aristocracy.*

TOWARDS the end of his *Brutus* Cicero remarks that none of his rivals in the forum were men of really wide culture: none but himself had the necessary familiarity with Greek and Roman literature; none had studied philosophy, jurisprudence, and history; none had fully mastered the technique of rhetorical style and composition.[1] The statement is obviously too sweeping to be taken literally; but it must have been true of many who, like Hortensius, relied chiefly on their natural talent for success in the forum.[2] On the other hand, no period in Roman history was so genuinely imbued with Greek culture at its best as the last century of the Republic. Sulla, Lucullus, Julius Caesar, Sallust, Cato, Varro, Brutus, Atticus, Servius Sulpicius, Cornelius Nepos: these are all names which recall, hardly less than the great names of Scipio's generation, what Cicero meant by his phrase *politior humanitas.* Almost without exception, too, they are names belonging to one or other of the great Roman *gentes*; and the connexion between the culture and the ancestry of these men,

[1] *Brut.* 322. [2] *ibid.* 320 foll.

among whom Cicero was and knew himself to be a *novus homo*, recalls the essentially Roman character of their *humanitas*.

Outside this exclusive Roman aristocracy the influence of Greek philosophy and Greek literature was less potent; the days of Marius and his imitators were definitely at an end. Caesar was now the acknowledged head of the democratic party, and the young men whom he gathered round him—Mark Antony, Dolabella, Curio, Caelius, and Sallust, for example—were very different from the men whose interests had been catered for by Plotius Gallus. Nor was rhetoric the only Greek study which had increased its popularity since the days of Marius. The first Latin text-books of philosophy were being produced about this time, and it is worth noting that the Epicureans were here first in the field.[1] Cicero complains more than once of the harm which their text-books were doing in half-educated circles; but Lucretius, Virgil, and Horace, all of them plebeians by birth, are no bad specimens of Epicurean teaching.[2]

The generation of Cicero and his contemporaries merges almost imperceptibly into the Augustan age, and the culture of the great Augustans is in a sense the autumn of Ciceronian *humanitas*. Livy is perhaps the best type of this new Ciceronianism, with his reverence for Roman traditions and his quick responsive-

[1] *Tusc.* iv. 6; *Acad.* i. 5; Schanz, i. 2, p. 339.

[2] Frank, pp. 48 foll.; Norden in *Neue Jahrb. für das klass. Altertum*, vol. vii, 1 (1901), p. 270.

ness to the Greek ideal. For Livy was not merely a historian. A keen student of both rhetoric and philosophy, he wrote philosophical dialogues which Seneca describes as more historical than philosophical;[1] and he dedicated an essay on rhetoric to his son, with the advice that he should remain faithful to the traditions of Demosthenes and Cicero.[2] But the contrast between Livy's elaborate periods and the more vigorous energy of Cicero's style is characteristic of a subtle change in the moral atmosphere of Rome. For whilst Livy and Cicero have in common their love for Greek thought and literature and their reverence for the glories of ancient Rome, the historian has learnt to look back on these glories as an achievement which can never be repeated; turning more and more from the present to the past, and looking forward to the future with something more than the apprehension of Cicero's later days. The same half-conscious pessimism is present even in the most confidently optimistic passages of Virgil's *Aeneid*. Cicero died without leaving a successor, and it was to be the same with both Virgil and Livy.

Meanwhile a greater than Livy was using his influence to maintain the traditions of Ciceronian *humanitas*. In his life of Cicero, Plutarch tells a story of the emperor Augustus which illustrates the dead orator's influence on the Augustan age.[3] Many years

[1] Sen. *Epp.* 100, 9; Hirzel, ii, p. 21.
[2] Quint. x. 1, 39; viii. 2, 18.
[3] Plut. *Cic.* 49; Zielinski, pp. 9 foll.

after Cicero's death one of the emperor's grandsons was reading a work by Cicero, possibly one of the *Philippics*. Augustus entered unexpectedly and the boy, startled at his approach, hid the book in the folds of his tunic. Augustus had seen the movement: taking the book from his grandson, he opened it and stood reading for some time. Then he handed it back with the words: 'A great intellect, my child; a great intellect and a true patriot.' The story may be an invention; or, if true, may well have been circulated by the emperor himself to make men forget the manner of Cicero's death. It is none the less significant. Cicero's influence could not be ignored, least of all by the man responsible for his murder.

And, apart from memories of personal antagonism, the emperor's Ciceronianism was no pose: his culture was the true Ciceronian *humanitas*. A literary purist in his style, he probably had studied in the school of some Alexandrian *grammaticus*: all the more so because his great-uncle, Julius Caesar, was a champion of the Analogists.[1] His teachers of rhetoric, Suetonius tells us, were M. Epidius and Apollodorus of Pergamon, one a Roman, the other a Greek;[2] and, just as Cicero had made Diodotus his constant companion and adviser, so Augustus kept his tutor Arius Didymus and his two sons Dionysius and Nicanor, as members of the imperial household.[3] Nor does the parallelism with Cicero end

[1] Suet. *Jul.* 56; *Oct.* 8. [2] *ibid. Oct.* 84, 89; *Rhet.* 1, 4.
[3] *ibid. Oct.* 89; Gardthausen, i. 1, p. 50; iii. 1, p. 1313.

here. Augustus published late in life his *Exhortationes ad philosophiam*, most probably modelled, like Cicero's *Hortensius*, on the *Protrepticus* of Posidonius;[1] and his interest in Greek and Roman history is no less Ciceronian.

> 'Nothing in his reading', says Suetonius, 'interested him so much as precepts or examples which might be of use in his private or public life. He had the habit of copying these out in full and sending them to his friends or to officials such as the generals of his armies, the governors of his provinces, the magistrates of Rome, whoever he thought stood in need of advice.'[2]

One name mentioned by Suetonius in his list of the future emperor's tutors deserves fuller notice. Apollodorus of Pergamon is named by Quintilian as the founder of an important school of rhetoric;[3] and there is good reason for attributing to his influence that school of 'Atticist' purism in literary style to which Brutus, Sallust, Octavian, and Pollio belonged, and against which Cicero defends his own 'Rhodian' style in the *Brutus* and *Orator*.[4] The controversy has no permanent importance in the history of Roman education, but it accounts for one curious personal episode in the history of Cicero's influence on the Augustan age. Asinius Pollio is in many ways the most outstanding literary figure of his generation, and he was certainly the direct inheritor of Cicero's literary traditions. Like Sallust, he was a Caesarian in politics and an Atticist in his

[1] Suet. *Oct.* 85; Hirzel, ii, p. 2.
[2] Suet. *Oct.* 89.
[3] Quint. iii. 1, 17.
[4] Schanz in *Hermes*, vol. xxv (1890), pp. 36–54; Wilamowitz, *ibid.*, vol. xxxv (1900), p. 46.

oratorical style, and must somehow or another have wounded Cicero's vanity: for the most biting sarcasms in the *Orator* are directed against the two Atticist historians.[1] Pollio retorted by an unsparing attack on Cicero's memory in his history of the civil wars,[2] and the feud was carried on by his son who wrote a book on the subject.[3] A delightful scene described by the elder Seneca puts the whole episode in its proper light. Messalla, one of Pollio's rivals in the forum and himself a distinguished orator of Cicero's school, had invited Pollio to a recitation in his house. A Spanish poet from Corduba was to read a poem on Cicero's death, and began his recitation with the pompous hexameter:

Conticuit Latiae tristis facundia linguae.

Pollio at once got up from his seat and left the room. 'You may do what you like in your own house, Messalla," he said, 'but I am not prepared to listen to a man who thinks me dumb.'[4]

Pollio was an influential personage in literary circles, and his anti-Ciceronian attitude may have helped to turn the younger generation away from Ciceronian traditions;[5] but the causes of reaction lay deeper. The fall of the Republic and the consequent loss of freedom in public life brought about a sudden drop in Roman traditions of citizenship which cannot be ignored, and new standards are apparent in Roman education as in everything else.

[1] *Or.* 30–2; Zielinski, p. 33. [2] Sen. *Suas.* 6, 14, 24–5.
[3] Plin. *Epp.* vii. 4, 3; Suet. *Claud.* 41.
[4] Sen. *Suas.* 6, 27. [5] Zielinski, pp. 33 foll.

'Our young men have grown slothful', says the elder Seneca, writing at the end of the Augustan age; 'their talents are left idle, and there is not a single honourable occupation for which they will toil day and night. Slumber and languor, and an interest in evil which is worse than slumber and languor, have entered into men's hearts. They sing and dance and grow effeminate, and curl their hair, and learn womanish tricks of speech: they are as languid as women, and deck themselves with unbecoming ornaments. Which of your contemporaries [he is addressing his three sons] has any talent, any industry? Which of them is in any way a man? Without strength, without energy, they add nothing during life to the gifts with which they were born, and then they complain of their lot. God forbid that the gift of eloquence should be given to their like!' [1]

The passage is rhetorical, but Seneca is writing of what he had seen; and there is other evidence of the same sort. It is perhaps forcing a point to take the contrast between Cicero's student-days and the student-days of his son as typical of the general change; but the experience of father and son is so curiously modern that some at least of the details must be quoted. They belong to a period more than half a century earlier than the date of Seneca's *Controversiae*.

Two years before his death Cicero sent his son for a couple of years to Athens, there to study rhetoric and philosophy, as he himself had done. We still have the letters in which he arranges with Atticus for a proper financial allowance to be paid his son at regular intervals.[2] 'See that he has everything he wants', the orator writes. 'I regard it as a question

[1] Sen. *Contr.* i, *praef.* 8–9.

[2] *ad Att.* xii. 24; xiv. 7, 2; 11, 2; 17, 5; xv. 15, 4; xvi. 1, 5.

of our good name and dignity as well as a duty: you will agree, I am sure.'[1] Then there is an interval without news. The boy is not writing home, and one of his tutors has sent an unsatisfactory report: Cicero begins to think that he had better go over to Athens himself.[2] The political situation here changes suddenly: Cicero is called to Rome, and the journey is off.[3] But his protests have had their effect. Young Marcus writes at last to his father: such an affectionate and elegantly worded letter that his father is sure all must be well.[4] And Trebonius, a friend who has been to Athens, writes that Cicero's son is hard at work, is the most pleasant young man in all Athens, and is very anxious to make a trip to Asia in company with Trebonius and his tutor Cratippus.[5] Cicero's correspondence was edited by Tiro after the orator's death, and Tiro must have chuckled as he added to the collection a letter which he himself had received from Marcus a few months later. After a few words of thanks for letters received by the last post, it continues as follows:

'I am sure, my dearest Tiro, that the reports about me which reach you answer your best wishes and hopes. I will make them good, and will do my best that this beginning of a good report may be daily repeated. So you may with perfect confidence fulfil your promise of being the trumpeter of my reputation. For the errors of my youth have caused me so much remorse and suffering that it is not only my heart that shrinks from what I did—my very ears abhor the mention of it. I know for a fact that you have shared my trouble and sorrow, and I don't wonder:

[1] *ad Att.* xiv. 7, 2. [2] *ibid.* xiv. 16, 3. [3] *ibid.* xvi. 7, 1.
[4] *ibid.* xv. 16; 17, 2. [5] *ad Fam.* xii. 16.

you always wished me to do well, not for my sake only but for your own. So as I have been the means of giving you pain, I will now take care that you shall feel double joy on my account.'

And the rest of the letter is a description of his virtuous conduct. Cratippus is a real father to him: 'I enjoy his lectures, but I am especially charmed by his delightful manners.' He is practising declamation every day, both in Greek and Latin; and has been careful to drop a tutor who was not to his father's liking. Of course there is a little occasional fun; but that 's to be expected. And he ends by poking some quiet fun at Tiro himself: 'How clearly I see your dearest face before me at this moment! I can see you buying things for the farm, talking to your bailiff, saving the seeds at dessert in your cloak.' [1]

Alas for the vanity of good resolutions! Tiro knew well what had happened to Marcus when he published that letter. 'Don't doubt, my dear Tiro', the boy had written, 'about my helping you in the future, if fortune will but stand by me.' Fortune failed Cicero's son as she failed so many of his friends and political allies. When next we hear of Marcus, he is a young man about town after the manner of Ovid, chiefly famous for his drinking bouts. 'There was nothing of the father in him', says the elder Seneca, 'save his wit.' [2]

The class most affected by this decline in the sense of civic responsibility was, of course, precisely the

[1] *ad Fam.* xvi. 21; Warde Fowler (*Social Life*, pp. 200–3) gives a translation of the whole text.

[2] Sen. *Suas.* 7, 13.

class for which Cicero had written his *de Oratore*: the ideal of the *doctus orator* lost half its meaning when public oratory ceased to be a main factor in Roman political life. One symptom of the loss to Roman education caused by these changed circumstances has often been overlooked. The old custom of the *tirocinium fori* was a valuable element in Roman education, even as late as the end of the Republic. Cicero himself gave others the benefit of his experience in this way, and young Caelius was one of those who got their first lessons in political life from the great orator.[1] But the fall of the Republic made the *tirocinium fori* an idle pretence, for the forum was now no longer the centre of Roman life. Its place was taken by a ceremonial entry on public life, apparently connected with the putting on of the *toga virilis*. Augustus, a conservative in all externals, made much of this ceremony, and had himself nominated consul for the two years in which he introduced his grandsons, Gaius and Lucius, to the forum.[2] Tiberius went through the same ceremony for his son Drusus,[3] and Claudius made Nero's *tirocinium fori* the occasion of a largess to the people and the army.[4] Nor was the ceremony confined to the imperial family, for Seneca mentions it as a regular feature of Roman life.[5] But it was a ceremony, and no more. In his *Dialogue on Orators* Tacitus speaks of the old custom as a thing of the past.

[1] Cic. *pro Cael.* 9. [2] Suet. *Oct.* 26; *Mon. Anc.* 3, 3.
[3] *ibid. Tib.* 15. [4] *ibid. Nero*, 7. [5] Sen. *Epp.* 4, 2.

'In the days of our ancestors', he says, 'if a young man was being prepared for the forum and public oratory, once he had been given the ordinary home-education and had mastered all the liberal arts (*honesta studia*), he was brought by his father or his relatives to the most distinguished orator in Rome. By following him about and mixing with his company the young man had an opportunity of listening to all his speeches in the law-courts or at a public meeting; and by hearing his patron in a debate or fighting a legal case he learnt how to bear himself in the fray.' [1]

Tacitus goes on to explain all the advantages such a system had for a young man who wished to be an orator: there was the added advantage of association with some of Rome's leading citizens. The new *tirocinium fori* lacked this element of personal contact. In the allusion which Seneca makes to the custom, he talks of the young man's pride in his new state, but there is not a word about the patron who performed the ceremony of introduction: [2] a significant contrast with Cicero's reminiscences of the Scaevolae.[3] Those who wanted to learn from the leading speakers in the forum were thus thrown back on their own resources, and it became a custom for students of rhetoric to go down themselves to the forum and listen to whatever speech attracted their attention. Quintilian commends this practice in his *Institutio oratoria*; [4] and Tacitus has a vivid description of these young students, note-book in hand, eager to scribble down any particularly brilliant *sententia* or point out to foreign visitors their favourite orator.[5] Tacitus himself listened as a

[1] Tac. *Dial.* 34. [2] Sen. *Epp.* 4, 2. [3] Cic. *de Am.* 1.
[4] Quint. x. 5, 19. [5] Tac. *Dial.* 20, 7, 10.

student to Aper, whom he was later to immortalize in his *Dialogue*, and visited him in his home;[1] and Pliny was among the young men who crowded to hear the 'stately' oratory of Tacitus.[2] But neither Tacitus nor Pliny received that intimate personal guidance which Cicero owed to the two Scaevolae.

§ 2. *New Elements in Roman Society.*

The students whom Tacitus describes in his *Dialogue* were mainly visitors from the provinces, most of them from Gaul and Spain;[3] and the fact is significant of a vast change that was taking place in Roman society under the early Empire. In a famous passage of his *Annals* Tacitus has analysed this social change, and has described the various elements which were rapidly replacing the old Roman aristocratic families in the senate and as officers of the imperial administration.[4] Two main types can be distinguished, each with its own particular needs in the sphere of education: the members of obscure Roman or Italian families who—'by good luck or by hard work', as Tacitus phrases it—had won an honourable place in the new régime; and an increasingly large body of talented provincials, to whom the imperial policy gave opportunities of public service which had been denied by the more conservative statesmen of the Republic. Both types are best studied in concrete examples.

[1] Tac. *Dial.* 2.
[2] Plin. *Epp.* vii. 20, 4; ii. 11, 17.
[3] Tac. *Dial.* 10, 20.
[4] Tac. *Ann.* iii. 55.

Vespasian is named by Tacitus as the man who did more than any one else to stem the tide of luxury and to bring Roman society back to something like its old simplicity:[1] his story is the story of a successful civil servant owing everything to the Empire. His grandfather had been a centurion in Pompey's army, his great-grandfather a contractor of slave-labour in Cisalpine Gaul; his father was a tax-farmer who had left a name for honesty in Asia Minor and Switzerland, and had married the daughter of a successful Roman officer. The only one of the future emperor's relatives who had attained senatorial rank was his mother's brother, who had been praetor, presumably under Augustus.[2] Vespasian himself began life as a *tribunus militum* in Thrace, was then quaestor in Crete or Cyrene, aedile and praetor in Rome, commanded an army first on the Rhine and then in Britain, and governed the province of Africa. Henceforth he was a marked man, though few even of his friends can have expected what did in fact happen. And what of his education? According to Suetonius, Vespasian was brought up by his grandmother on a farm near Reate.[3] Horace describes how 'the big sons of big centurions' went every day to school at Venusia;[4] and Vespasian, the grandson of a retired centurion, must have gone to school with his like. Persius is fond of quoting such retired centurions as the type of rough, uncultured country-folk,[5] and it is not surprising to read in Suetonius

[1] *ibid., loc. cit.* [2] Suet. *Vesp.* 1. [3] *ibid.* 2.
[4] Hor. *Serm.* i. 6, 72. [5] Pers. *Sat.* iii. 77; v. 189.

that to the end of his life Vespasian never got rid of his country accent.[1] Yet somewhere or other he had been to school with a Greek *grammaticus*, for later in life he surprised his courtiers by the readiness with which he could quote Homer and Menander.[2] Possibly his mother's relatives had sent him to school at Rome: just as Horace's freedman father brought his boy up to the city from Venusia and sent him to a school where he learnt lessons 'which any Roman knight or senator might teach his children'.[3] That is all we know; but the regular age for 'taking a commission' as *tribunus militum* was eighteen,[4] and once begun Vespasian's official career was never interrupted.

Good luck and hard work were both conspicuous in Vespasian's career, but he is the type of hundreds of other civil servants and military men whose names have perished, or have survived only on some official inscription. The younger Pliny's correspondents, with their endless talk of culture and literary criticism, were the sons and grandsons of men like Vespasian: some of them, like Terentius Junior whom Pliny visited at his farm one day and found full of interest in Greek literature,[5] were themselves retired civil servants with records not unlike Vespasian's before the year of the four emperors. And it is Pliny who makes the remark: 'How many well-read men are forgotten by the world, thanks to

[1] Suet. *Vesp.* 22. [2] *ibid.* 23. [3] Hor. *Serm.* i. 6, 77.
[4] Cagnat in Daremberg-Saglio, iii. 2, p. 1053.
[5] Pliny, *Epp.* vii. 25.

their modesty and retiring life!'[1] One other sentence from Pliny's correspondence is worth quoting for the experience which it reflects. 'My young friend', he writes in a letter of introduction, 'is of an excellent family and has all the talents needed for success: he is fond of study, like most poor men.'[2] Cicero's father might have introduced his son to Scaevola with the same words.

The imperial civil service, which usually implied service as an officer in the army, was perhaps the surest road to success under the early Empire. Nowadays we should naturally add the learned professions, but Roman society looked down on doctors and schoolmasters as semi-servile professions. Greek opinion was much the same. 'If there were no doctors', said a witty Greek proverb, 'there would be no greater fool than a schoolmaster';[3] and the two professions were for the most part left to Greek freedmen. 'Make your son an auctioneer or an architect rather than a schoolmaster', says Martial to a Roman parent;[4] and Juvenal associates doctors and schoolmasters with painters, attendants at the public baths, fortune-tellers, and tight-rope dancers.[5] There remained the legal profession with its various branches; the advocate (*patronus*, *advocatus*, or *causidicus*), the notary (*notarius*), the lawyer (*pragmaticus*) who got up the legal facts for the advocate, and the assistant-magistrate (*assessor*)

[1] *ibid.* vii. 25, 1. [2] *ibid.* vii. 22, 2.
[3] Athenaeus, xv. 666 A; Blümner, p. 476.
[4] Mart. v. 56. [5] Juv. iii. 76.

who sat with the praetor or governor in the courts.[1] Under the Empire this was the favourite, as well as the most specialized, learned profession; and a conventional *declamatio* in the schools of rhetoric, hardly less trite than the comparison between town-life and country-life, was the choice between life as a lawyer or soldier.[2]

Those who wished to devote their lives to a serious study of law attended a regular course of lectures given in public by some distinguished *iurisperitus.*[3] Under the Empire recognized schools of law came into existence, not only in Rome but also in the provinces, notably at Berytus in Phoenicia. At Rome the two most famous schools were the Sabiniani and the Proculiani, and the Digest gives a list of the successive heads of each school, beginning with Ateius Capito and Antistius Labeo.[4] But these schools were attended for the most part by students who hoped to become in turn either *assessores* or *iurisperiti*, both of them highly specialized professions. The more ambitious preferred the career of advocate in the courts, where reputations were more easily made. No special studies were needed for this career, no talent save the artificial eloquence of the period; for the *pragmaticus* was always at hand with his legal notes on the case, and the universal habit of bribing both judge and advocate made the profession

[1] Friedlaender, i, pp. 185 foll. (i, p. 334).

[2] Quint. ii. 4, 24.

[3] Bremer, pp. 7 foll.

[4] *Dig.* ii. 1, 2, 47 foll.; Bremer, pp. 68 foll.

singularly lucrative.[1] An incident which occurred in A.D. 47, during the reign of Claudius, will illustrate the new surroundings to which Cicero's *doctus orator* had perforce to adapt himself.

Claudius was, according to Tacitus, a weak emperor, and his policy had allowed grave abuses to become the rule in the courts of law. Spying by paid informers (*delatio*) had become a fine art, and the worst offenders were advocates who brought forward an accusation simply for the sake of blackmail. In self-defence the senatorial party demanded a reform. Under the Republic the *lex Cincia*, passed in 204 B.C., had forbidden advocates to accept payment, and Augustus had reinforced the law by a severe penalty.[2] But this penalty was ignored in practice, and the motion brought forward by the consul designate for A.D. 47 was simply that the penalties prescribed by Augustus should be put into force. Tacitus summarizes the debate that followed, and it is clear that the struggle was between two social orders.[3] On the one hand, an appeal was made to Roman traditions. Eloquence had once been the first of the liberal arts: now it was but the instrument of a sordid trade. The reply was obvious. Times had changed since the days of Cicero and Hortensius, or even Pollio and Messalla. Oratory was now a profession, and advocates were dependent on their fees. Many a poor man had made his name in the forum of recent years,

[1] Friedlaender, i, pp. 182 foll. (i, p. 330).

[2] Tac. *Ann.* xi. 5; Dio, xliv. 18; Klingmüller in Pauly-Wissowa, viii. 2274.

[3] Tac. *Ann.* xi. 5–7.

but a revival of the obsolete sanction would place an unjust premium on the possession of private means. Claudius took the democratic side, and contented himself with placing a reasonable limit on the fees an advocate might receive; and in spite of an attempt made by Nero to revive the *lex Cincia* in the first year of his reign, this compromise remained a permanent part of Roman law.[1] A generation later Quintilian boasts that no more honourable profession than the advocate's is to be found in Rome.[2]

This professional class of which Tacitus and Quintilian speak was not the only new element in Roman society under the early Empire. So fantastic are the stories told by Tacitus, Suetonius, Martial, and Juvenal of the freedmen who made their fortunes under Tiberius, Claudius, and Nero that one hesitates before counting these men as a normal element of any society. Yet the evidence of such inscriptions as have been collected and classified shows that the despised freedman, usually of Eastern descent, was steadily coming to the front in Roman society, even as early as the first century A.D.[3] And no account of Roman life under the early Empire is complete without the evidence of Petronius. One of Trimalchio's boon-companions airs his views on education in a speech which deserves to be quoted in full. A teacher of rhetoric is present at the famous banquet,

[1] Tac. *Ann.* xiii. 5; Plin. *Epp.* v. 9 (21), 4; *Dig.* i. 13, 1, 10–13; xviii. 1, 7.

[2] Quint. xii. 7, 10.

[3] See an able article by Prof. Tenney Frank on 'Race Mixture in the Roman Empire' (*Amer. Hist. Review* (1916), pp. 689–708).

and the speaker has been irritated by the schoolmaster's sneers at the bad Latin he was hearing all round him.[1]

'You think I'm an old chatterbox, Agamemnon; but why don't you answer me, you who've been taught to make speeches? You're not one of us, and that 's why you laugh at us poor folk when we open our mouths. We all know you're mad on books. But come over to my farm some day, and I'll show you my little cottage. You'll get something to eat there: chickens, eggs, something worth eating, even though the weather has turned everything topsy-turvy this year. And I've got a young boy who would make a good pupil for you. He has learnt simple division already, and you may have him as a servant-boy yet, if he lives. For he never has his head out of a book, if you give him a minute to spare. He 's clever and a good lad, but he 's crazy on birds. I've killed three of his goldfinches already, and told him it was the weasel that ate them. But now he 's got a new fad and will do nothing but paint. However, he has begun his Greek at last, and is beginning to like his Latin, though his master is a conceited fellow who is never quiet at any job I give him, but comes and asks for something to copy, and then won't do his own work. I've got another boy too, but he 's no scholar. He 's anxious to learn, however, and is getting along faster than he thinks. He comes home every holiday and takes whatever you give him. So I've bought the lad some of those red-letter books, for I want him to learn some law and be able to keep himself. That 's the job that pays. For he 's got education enough for his age. If he cries off, I've made up my mind to teach him a trade. We'll make him a barber or an auctioneer, or at the worst an advocate. Then he 's safe for life. So I keep telling him every day: Believe me, my boy, whatever you learn is all for the good. Look at the advocate Phileros. If he hadn't learnt his lessons, he'd go hungry to-day. It 's not so long since he was carrying sacks to market on his back, and now he 's able to hold his own against Norbanus. Education is a gold-mine, my boy, and a trade sticks to you for life.'

The last phrase deserves to be quoted in the original:

[1] Petron. *Sat.* 46.

'Litterae thesaurum est, et artificium nunquam moritur.' It is a fitting counterpart to Trimalchio's self-chosen epitaph: 'He began life as a poor man, died a millionaire, and never listened to a lecture on philosophy.'[1]

None of these new elements in Roman society was likely to find Cicero's *politior humanitas* a practicable ideal. But the admission of men from the provinces to a full share in the political and social life of Rome had an even more decisive influence on the future character of Roman education. The term 'provincial' is not very easy to define, for it covers citizens from the older Roman colonies in the provinces as well as Gauls and Spaniards whose fathers or grandfathers had fought against Rome. As a rule we know no more of a 'provincial' than the town at which he was born. The Senecas, for example, and Porcius Latro came from Corduba, Quintilian from Calagurris, Martial from Bilbilis, and Domitius Afer from Nemausus; but that is all we know. Sometimes we know even less: M. Aper, for example, was a Gaul, but his birthplace is unknown. Generalizations where so little is certain are not very trustworthy, but Tacitus expressly names the 'new men (*novi homines*) from the municipalities and colonies and even the provinces' as a chief factor in the new social life of Rome: 'they brought with them', he says, 'the frugal habits of their homes, and kept the old spirit even when, by good luck or hard work, they had acquired wealth for their old age.'[2]

[1] Petron. *Sat.* 71.

[2] Tac. *Ann.* iii. 55.

Two tendencies seem to have been generally characteristic of these provincials. One was a more than Roman consciousness of their status as Roman citizens, with a more than Roman pride in the language and literature of Rome. This tendency had been noticeable as early as the days of Cicero. 'Our citizens', says Crassus in the *de Oratore*, 'are less interested in literature than the Latins.'[1] Only now the place of the Latins is taken by natives of the great Western provinces, notably Spain and Gaul: Quintilian a Spaniard, definitely counts all Italy as Roman in the matter of correct Latin speech.[2] And just as Rome had drawn all the talent of Latium to its schools, so now students from Italy and all the provinces flock to the capital. Virgil, for example, came up from the schools of Cremona and Milan at the age of fifteen;[3] Horace as a boy from Venusia, where his father would not allow him to attend the local school;[4] Persius from Volaterrae at the age of twelve.[5] Cisalpine Gaul (*Gallia togata*) was especially noted for its schools; Suetonius says that there were distinguished Latin *grammatici* in that province as early as the first century B. C.[6] Transalpine Gaul was quick to follow this example, and the list of Gauls who made their names as orators in Rome during the first century A. D.—Domitius Afer, Montanus, Florus, and M. Aper—justifies Juvenal's epithet, *Gallia facunda*.[7]

[1] Cic. *de Or.* iii. 43.
[2] Quint. i. 5, 56.
[3] *Vit. Donat.*; Frank, pp. 16 foll.
[4] Hor. *Serm.* i. 6, 72 foll.
[5] *Vit. Pers.*; Schanz, ii. 2, p. 80.
[6] Suet. *Gram.* 3.
[7] Juv. xv. 111.

Spain has an even more distinguished list, and it is interesting to note the Roman mentality of these 'Spanish' authors. Quintilian, for example, who was born in Spain and had begun his work as teacher and advocate there, quotes a Latin word—*gurdus*—with the remark: 'I am told that this word, which is vulgarly used instead of *stolidus*, is of Spanish origin.'[1] And Martial's praise of Bilbilis shows that his birthplace was an entirely Latin town;[2] whilst the verses he sends to a lady-friend, Marcella, who had presented him with a comfortable estate in Bilbilis, are delightful in their snobbery. 'Who would think that you live in a Spanish town', he writes to her, 'or that you were born in such surroundings? Your taste is so rare, so exquisite, that no lady born in the Suburra or on the Capitoline is your rival.'[3] Poor Marcella must have worked hard to earn that praise, if it was her due: for Cicero pokes fun at the Latin of Corduba,[4] and Porcius Latro, a native of that town, could never get rid of his Spanish style.[5] But Seneca, Quintilian, and Martial all write Latin as to the manner born, and many of their countrymen must have envied them their *os Latinum*, to use Pliny's phrase.[6] For no province was more eager than Spain to acquire Roman habits; and Pliny notes the Spanish reputation for a peculiarly Roman quality, *gravitas*.[7]

[1] Quint. i. 5, 57; see also, i. 5, 8.
[2] Mart. i, 61; xii. 18.
[3] *ibid.* xii. 21, 31.
[4] Cic. *pro Arch.* 26.
[5] Sen. *Suas.* 6, 27; *Contr.* i, *praef.* 16.
[6] Pliny, *Epp.* vi. 11, 2.
[7] *ibid* ii. 13, 4.

The other tendency which characterizes almost all these provincial writers is a passion for rhetoric ; and here the phenomenon is less easily explained. Possibly it was their lack of mastery over the finer cadences of Latin verse and prose ; for rhetoric is the most obvious of literary forms, and the most easily acquired. But, whatever the cause, there can be no mistaking the general drift of Latin literature at this period. Seneca, Lucan, Persius, Statius, Porcius Latro, and the whole tribe of *rhetores* : these are the outstanding names, and they are one and all monotonous in their declamatory vehemence. The greatest of them are Spaniards, and a generalization is easily made. But there were other declaimers as well as they, and one name is sufficient to redeem the province's reputation. Quintilian was a Spaniard, and his *Institutio oratoria* contains the sanest criticism ever written of all this new-fangled rhetoric.

§ 3. *Education of the Lower Classes.*

Modern experience would suggest that a generation which saw the transition from a conservative aristocracy to a society mainly composed of the professional middle-class would be noted for its practical standards of education. Yet Cicero's *politior humanitas* is less academic than the ἐγκύκλιος παιδεία of Vitruvius and Quintilian, and there is no trace of a struggle between what we should now call the Humanist tradition and any more ' scientific ' type of school studies. Even in Hellenistic Greece, where the scientific spirit was incomparably more vigorous than it ever was under the Roman Empire, Greek instincts for order and harmony kept the mere thirst for knowledge in check; and the *ἐγκύκλιος παιδεία* described by Quintilian is essentially Hellenistic in its origin and spirit. In Rome the scientific spirit was never strong. Grammar and jurisprudence are the only two sciences in which Roman scholars did original work, and even here their work was directly inspired by Hellenistic scholarship and Hellenistic philosophy. As for the mathematical and applied sciences, Pliny's *Natural History* and Seneca's *Quaestiones naturales* show how far the Romans were from original research-work in these fields. No Roman writer ever thought of giving his public more than a popular account of Greek scientific theories and discoveries; the Roman Empire never produced a scientific discovery that has been of permanent use to mankind. Architecture is the one branch of applied mathematics in which they showed real genius: yet Roman architects were always dependent on Greek theory for their practical work. Vitruvius, whose own work is merely an intelligent compilation from earlier Greek sources, complains that the Romans had produced no technical literature of their profession comparable in bulk or quality with the text-books of Greek specialists.[1]

Vitruvius tells us in his preface that he is writing as an architect for architects,[2] and the statement

[1] Vitruv. vii, *praef.* 14; Schanz, ii. 1, p. 539.
[2] Vitruv. i. 1, 18.

makes his theory of education all the more interesting. No student of architecture, he says, should come to the profession without an adequate general education: he must be able to read and write and draw, and have also studied geometry, optics, arithmetic, history, philosophy, music, medicine, law, and astronomy.[1] This is, of course, with certain modifications, the ordinary Hellenistic ἐγκύκλιος παιδεία, and Vitruvius himself uses the term (*encyclios disciplina*).[2] Some of the objects included in this programme have no apparent connexion with architecture, and it is amusing to see how Vitruvius tries to justify his theory. Music, for example, must be studied because certain tuning instruments were used by architects to test the accuracy of their calculations; philosophy gives knowledge of the physical sciences, and also teaches generosity and commercial honesty; law may be useful in professional litigation; and history will help an intelligent architect to explain the meaning of his designs—why he designs Caryatid statues, for example.[3]

All this is given with a mixture of Greek terminology—*graphis*, *euthygramma*, *physiologia*, *hemitonia*, *symphonia*, *clima*, *encyclios*, *agrammatos*, *amusos*, *aniatrologetos*, and so forth—which warns us that Vitruvius is borrowing his arguments from some Greek source; and the underlying principle of all his theory is plainly Greek. 'Every science (*ars*)',

[1] *ibid.* i. 1, 3.
[2] *ibid.* i. 1, 12; vi, *praef.* 4; see above, p. 85.
[3] Vitruv. i. 1, 4–10.

he says, 'is composed of two elements, practice (*opus*) and theory (*ratiocinatio*). The former is peculiar to trained specialists in each science; the latter is common to all educated men (*docti*).'[1] This is the principle which underlies Cicero's theory of the *doctus orator*, and it is no chance coincidence that Vitruvius repeats in this context another of Cicero's favourite theories, that all the sciences (*artes*) are linked together in one vast system.[2] Cicero was a specialist in his own profession as well as a man of universal culture; and that is precisely what Vitruvius means by his *encyclios disciplina*. He himself was no mere theorist, but a practical business man, who had received a good technical training in his profession and had since then acquired considerable personal experience.[3] The conclusion would seem to be obvious that the theory of education which he propounds was common to men of his type. Not that all architects were as well educated as Vitruvius, any more than all orators were as well educated as Cicero. But the ἐγκύκλιος παιδεία was plainly an accepted standard of education: a purely professional education would have been considered 'illiberal'.

In his *de Officiis* Cicero ranks architecture (which for the Romans included engineering) together with medicine and school-mastering as beneath the liberal professions, but above such 'sordid trades' as

[1] Vitruv. i. 1, 15.

[2] *Ibid.* i. 1, 12; Cic. *de Or.* iii. 21; see above, p. 89.

[3] Vitruv. i. 1, 2; iv. 3, 3; vi, *praef.* 4; x. 11, 2.

cooking, dancing, shopkeeping, and all forms of manual labour.[1] This classification helps to define the various grades into which the new Roman society was divided by social convention. The great mass of the Roman people were engaged in one or other of the 'sordid trades' which Cicero despised: for most of them the elementary schools of reading, writing, and arithmetic were more than sufficient. 'My parents were poor, ignorant folk', says a cobbler in one of Martial's epigrams; 'who taught me the A B C themselves. What have I to do with schools of literature and rhetoric?'[2] And one of the guests at Trimalchio's table boasts that he has not learnt 'geometry and literature and all the rest of that sort of nonsense, but can read the letters on an inscription, knows his weights and measures, and can add up any sum'.[3] Seneca calls such an education 'servile',[4] but many a free-born citizen probably got no further.

The more reputable professions mentioned by Cicero—medicine, engineering, and architecture—demanded a higher standard of education. The *encyclios disciplina* detailed by Vitruvius is too vague to be a sure guide; but some form of general education was plainly considered essential. Vitruvius includes philosophy and law in his list, and omits rhetoric. The omission is curious, though Vitruvius says nothing to explain it. Possibly the course of rhetoric which Cicero includes in his normal *puerilis*

[1] Cic. *de Off.* i. 151.
[2] Mart. ix. 73, 7.
[3] Petron. *Sat.* 58.
[4] Sen. *de Tran. an.* 9, 5.

institutio was not thought necessary for a practical profession such as architecture; but that is only a guess. Most architects and doctors probably went at least to the schools of the *grammaticus* and the *geometres*. When Vitruvius says that some of his profession were 'illiterate' (*sine litteris*),[1] he must mean that they had not been to a school of literature; and Galen complains a century later that medical quacks were going about the country who could barely read and write.[2]

Cicero ends his classification of the 'sordid' and 'liberal' professions with the remark: 'Of money-making professions none is better, more fruitful, more pleasant and more worthy of a free man than agriculture.'[3] This praise of agriculture, coming from such a lover of the city, sounds somewhat conventional. Columella, who was a farmer by profession as well as by choice, has a different story to tell, and his comment bears directly on the history of Roman education. He has been speaking of the steady decline in agriculture during the preceding hundred years, and this is his analysis of its cause.

'We should blame ourselves for our misfortunes, not nature or the climate. Our forefathers gave their best men and their best energies to the work of agriculture, but we leave it all to our worst slaves, as though it were work fit only for the public executioner. We are men of strange habits. When we want to learn oratory, we are careful to imitate the best orator. We go to school to learn our weights and measures. We study music,

[1] Vitruv. i. 1, 2.
[2] Galen, *de Propr. libr.* 9; Friedlaender, i, p. 192 (i, p. 343).
[3] Cic. *de Off.* i. 151.

song, dance, and gesture. When we want to build, we call in mason and architect. We have skilled captains for our ships, trained soldiers for our armies. We have specialists for every useful science, and we have philosophers to form our characters. Agriculture is the only science for which we have neither pupils nor masters; yet agriculture is the science next in dignity to philosophy, almost its sister-science. We have schools of rhetoric, schools of geometry, schools of music; trained cooks and trained barbers. But I never yet heard of men who call themselves students or professors of agriculture.' [1]

This plea for schools of agriculture sounds curiously modern and shows how far Roman society had drifted from the days of Cato and Varro. The evidence supplied by Columella himself and by the writers of the next generation shows that Roman methods of land-ownership were at this time passing through a period of transition.[2] In place of the old Roman farm owned and worked by a Roman citizen, vast estates (*latifundia*) had been formed in Italy and the provinces. These estates were held by men of property, who dwelt for the most part in cities, rarely or never visited their farms, but allowed them to be worked either by gangs of slaves under the management of a steward (*villicus*) or by small tenants (*coloni*) paying rent to their landlord. How far were the old traditions of Roman home-life maintained by these *coloni*? Evidence is lacking, but the letters of the younger Pliny leave a general impression of perpetual arrears and discontent. At

[1] Columella, i, *praef.* 1–7 (I have condensed the original).

[2] See the evidence collected by Heitland in his *Agricola* (Cambridge, 1921); especially the chapters on Columella, the younger Pliny, and the Inscriptions relative to *Alimenta*.

best, such tenants must have been without that pride in work done on their own farm which is so plain in the writings of Cato and Varro. The Roman state had definitely passed from the days of citizen-farmers and farmer-soldiers to the specialization and centralization inevitable in a more advanced stage of social development. Rome was now the centre of a great Empire and Roman society had perforce to adapt itself to changed conditions. Columella's is the only voice raised in protest against the literary education which this new society had adopted ; and his protest is not against the ἐγκύκλιος παιδεία as such, but against the exclusion of agriculture from the cycle of *artes liberales*.

VIII

THE NEW RHETORIC

'Non vitae, sed scholae discimus.' Sen. *Epp.* 106, 12.

§ 1. *Virgil and Horace in the Schools.*

THE list of *artes liberales* given by Vitruvius shows that the 'encyclic' programme was as indefinite in his day as in the days of Cicero and Varro. Optics certainly and drawing most probably were added by the architect for professional reasons: history should be counted as part of literature. This reduces the list to eight, and the addition of rhetoric, universally recognized as an *ars* and part of the 'encyclic' programme, brings the number to the nine mentioned by Cicero and Varro. But the absence of allusions to the work done by teachers of music and mathematics shows that literature, rhetoric, and philosophy were still the most important items of the programme. And here the evidence is abundant.

In theory at least the schools of literature continued to do the work described by Cicero in his *de Oratore.*[1] Seneca's description of the work done by a *grammaticus* is almost identical with Cicero's: 'The *grammaticus* is concerned with correctness of speech: with history, too, if he wishes to extend his domain; and, at the very furthest, with poetry.'[2]

[1] Cic. *de Or.* i. 187.

[2] Sen. *Epp.* 88, 3.

Allowing for the contempt which Seneca affects here and elsewhere [1] when speaking of the *grammatici*, these are the very functions ascribed by Cicero to the teacher of literature. But literature is more dependent than any other subject on the medium in which it is taught and the text-books used; and the generation which had lived since Cicero's death had changed the whole character of Roman literary education.

Suetonius says that it was Q. Caecilius Epirota, a freedman of Cicero's friend Atticus and an intimate friend of the poet Cornelius Gallus, who first commented in class on the works of Virgil and the other Augustan poets.[2] It would be hard to exaggerate the importance of this step. Hitherto the Roman schools of literature had taken their standards of excellence from Greek authors, even when the actual texts read at school were Latin. Now the Latin *grammaticus* was able to draw on a literature which was genuinely comparable with the classical literature of Greece, and which had the added advantage of being thoroughly national in its spirit. Virgil was accepted immediately as the national poet of Rome: Petronius calls him simply 'Roman Virgil'.[3] Horace's *Odes* were hardly less national, and they must have been the joy of schoolmasters from the first. But what was wanted was a poem which should tell the story of Roman greatness for Roman boys, and that is precisely the theme of Virgil's *Aeneid*. As Servius puts it in his commentary on the sixth book: 'An

[1] Sen. *Epp*. 58, 5; 108, 24 foll.
[2] Suet. *Gram*. 16.
[3] Petron. *Sat*. 118.

attentive examination will show that Virgil has commemorated in brief form all Roman history from the coming of Aeneas to his own day, a fact which is obscured by the broken order of his narrative.' [1] But a *grammaticus* who was interested in his work could easily make the *Aeneid* a text-book of Roman history up to the days of Augustus: Quintilian even complains that many *grammatici* gave too much attention to these historical and mythological details.[2] And Virgil was the happy hunting-ground of the grammarian as well as the antiquarian: his erudition was the delight of later scholars, and his authority, like Cicero's, was final in all questions of correct speech.[3]

It was thus inevitable that the example set by Caecilius should become the rule. Suetonius tells us that there was opposition at first, and Caecilius was lampooned as 'the nurse of our baby poets'. But another famous *grammaticus* of the Augustan age, C. Julius Hyginus, published a full commentary on Virgil's poems, which won him praise from Ovid as a 'zealous student of our modern poets'; [4] and other commentaries followed in the next generation, as well as a critical edition of both Virgil and Horace by Valerius Probus.[5] Henceforward the position of the two poets was undisputed. Quintilian and

[1] Serv. *ad Aen.* vi. 752; Comparetti, p. 11.

[2] Quint. i. 8, 18–21.

[3] Sen. *Epp.* 108, 24–35; Gell. v. 12, 13; Comparetti, pp. 29 foll.

[4] Ovid, *Trist.* iii. 14, 7; Schanz, ii. 1, p. 511.

[5] Schanz, ii. 1, pp. 117, 185.

Tacitus take it for granted that Virgil will be the first poet read in every Roman school, just as Homer was in Greece ; [1] and Juvenal has associated the names of Virgil and Horace with the oil and smoke of Roman class-rooms in verses that would have made Horace shudder to hear his worst forebodings trumpeted abroad as an accomplished fact.[2]

Virgil and Horace were not the only modern poets read in the schools of the early Empire. Suetonius expressly says that Caecilius lectured on Virgil ' and the other modern poets '. The phrase probably includes Horace and the elegiac poets. Ovid was hardly famous enough for this honour during the lifetime of Caecilius ; but somewhat later a teacher of rhetoric, Cestius Pius, had to rebuke his pupils for their imitation of Ovid's style.[3] Lucan was a school author almost within his lifetime : Suetonius read him at school, and Tacitus ranks him as a classic with Virgil and Horace.[4] Statius was even able to boast that his poems became school-texts immediately after they were published ; [5] and this tribute to the reputation of a living author must have been common enough, for both Persius and Martial refer to it as the final test of popularity.[6]

The schools of literature were thus in close touch with the literary fashions of the day, and more than

[1] Quint. i. 8, 5 ; x. 1, 86 ; Tac. *Dial.* 12.

[2] Juv. vii. 225 foll. ; Mart. v. 56 names Cicero and Virgil as typical school-texts.

[3] Sen. *Contr.* iii. Exc. 7.

[4] *Vita Lucani* ; Tac. *Dial.* 20.

[5] Stat. *Theb.* xii. 815.

[6] Pers. *Sat.* i. 29 ; Mart. viii. 3, 15.

one *grammaticus* made his mark in literary circles. Most famous of them all was Remmius Palaemon, author of the first Latin grammar ever published and teacher of both Persius and Quintilian.[1] His scholarship is only known to us by guesswork, but Suetonius gives us a good deal of unsavoury gossip about his personality.[2] He had started life as a slave, but won such a reputation for literary talent and erudition that in spite of gross personal immorality his class-room was the most fashionable in Rome. His *Ars Grammatica* was almost certainly the first of its kind, being a text-book of Latin grammar for use in schools, apparently modelled on the standard Greek grammar of Dionysius Thrax.[3] Its success was immediate, for Juvenal refers to it as a classic of his school-days, and it was much used by the later Latin grammarians.[4] Nor was Palaemon the man to underestimate the value of his wares. 'Latin scholarship was born with me, and will die with me', he was fond of saying; and he never called Varro, the greatest of Roman scholars, by any other name than 'The Pig'. Virgil was his favourite poet, largely for personal reasons. Palaemon appears as arbiter between two poets in one of the Eclogues; a plain prophecy that Palaemon would one day be the judge of all poets and poetry.[5]

[1] *Vita Persii*; schol. ad Juv. vi. 451; but see below, p. 181.

[2] Suet. *Gram.* 23; see also Pliny, *N.H.* xiv. 49–50 for a curious anecdote about Palaemon as a land-owner.

[3] Nettleship, *Essays* (Second Series), pp. 163 foll.

[4] Juv. vi. 452; Schanz, ii. 2, p. 431.

[5] Suet. *Gram.* 23.

§ 2. *The New Schools of Rhetoric.*

Suetonius tells us that both Tiberius and Claudius used their personal influence against the popularity of this amazing schoolmaster and failed. Other *grammatici* of the period—Verrius Flaccus, for example, Julius Hyginus and C. Melissus [1]—were high in the imperial favour, and it is plain that the teachers of literature were acquiring a new social standing in Rome. But the *grammatici* were far less popular than the contemporary teachers of rhetoric, and their class-rooms far less fashionable. Those who know the Augustan age only from the works of Virgil, Horace, Ovid, and Livy can form no true judgement of the literary society in which these stately ' Augustans ' moved. Fortunately Seneca's father, who was a student of rhetoric all his life and lived to the age of seventy, wrote down his personal reminiscences of the *rhetores* and their art for the benefit of his sons. These reminiscences contain an endless number of *sententiae*, *divisiones*, and *colores* which the old man had either learnt by heart or jotted down in his note-book.[2] They make dull reading enough ; but they are seasoned by criticisms and personal anecdotes, told for the most part in a conversational manner, and thrown into the form of a preface to each book of the collection. No student of the Augustan age should leave those prefaces unread.

Dates are here important, for without Seneca's

[1] Suet. *Gram.* 17, 20, 21.

[2] Sen. *Contr.* i, *praef.* 1–5.

formal testimony it would be hard to believe that these *sententiae* and *colores* were composed and admired within a few years of Cicero's death. Yet such is the fact. Were it not for the civil war between Caesar and Pompey, Seneca would have come as a boy from Spain to Rome in time to hear Cicero's last speeches ;[1] and the declamations from which he quotes were for the most part delivered during the next twenty or thirty years. Seneca himself speaks of these declamations as an entirely new fashion—'a thing born after me', to use his own phrase.[2] The statement needs to be qualified : for declamation was an exercise which the Gracchi had practised, and which Cicero kept up all his life. But the type of declamation which Seneca knew was wholly modern, in subject-matter and in style. No attempt can be made here to reproduce the style of these new *rhetores* with their never-ending *sententiae* and their amazing artificiality : but a few typical subjects may be quoted. They will show how far the schools of Latin rhetoric had drifted since the days of Plotius Gallus.

One of Seneca's *Controversiae*, for which he quotes specimens from all the leading *rhetores*, deals with the following imaginary plot : [3]

'The law requires that children should support their parents or be imprisoned. A man has slain one of his brothers as a tyrant and another because he was taken in adultery, though his father begged for mercy. The man is captured by pirates, who write to the father for a ransom. The father answers that he will pay

[1] *ibid.* i, *praef.* 11. [2] *ibid.* i, *praef.* 12. [3] *ibid.* i. 7.

them double if they will cut off his son's hands. The son is released by the pirates, and refuses to support his father.'

Another tells the story of a well-known romance : [1]

' A husband and wife have sworn that neither shall survive the other. The husband goes on a journey, and sends a messenger to his wife with news of his death. The wife leaps from a cliff, but is rescued and restored to health. She is ordered by her father to desert her husband, but refuses. She is disinherited.'

And another : [2]

' A young man is captured by pirates and writes to his father for the ransom. No ransom is sent. The daughter of the pirate-captain makes him swear that he will marry her if he is released. She elopes with him, and they return to the young man's home where they are married. A rich heiress crosses their path. The father bids the young man forsake his wife and marry the heiress. He refuses and is disinherited.'

And another : [3]

' During a civil war a woman follows her husband, though her father and brother are on the other side. Her husband's side is defeated and her husband killed. She returns to her father who will not receive her. She asks how she can win his favour, and he replies : "By dying." She hangs herself before his door. The father is accused of madness by his son.'

The subjects of the *Suasoriae* were more historical, and for that reason were less popular. Seneca gives us only seven examples : two about Alexander the Great, who deliberates whether he should cross the ocean that bounded the world, and whether he should enter Babylon in spite of omens and auguries ; two others about the Spartans at Thermopylae and the Athenians after Salamis ; another about Agamemnon and Iphigeneia ; and two about Cicero's

[1] Sen. *Contr.* ii. 2. [2] *ibid.* i. 6. [3] *ibid.* x. 3.

last hours. These last two are interesting for the light they throw on Cicero's personal influence a generation after his death. In both Cicero figures as the martyr of his eloquence. 'Should he ask Mark Antony for mercy?' 'Should he burn his writings as the price of safety?'[1] These are the questions discussed, and their development is obvious. But Cicero's name was not always held in such high honour by the *rhetores* and their pupils. It was apparently a common practice to compose declamations in answer to Cicero's speeches. Messalla and Pollio, for example, wrote speeches in defence of Catiline;[2] the *rhetor* Cestius Pius wrote an answer to Cicero's *pro Milone*;[3] and Brutus wrote a *pro Milone* of his own as a school exercise.[4] Sometimes these speeches were attributed to some well-known orator of Cicero's day: Asconius quotes two such speeches in answer to Cicero's *in Toga candida*, one attributed to Catiline, the other to C. Antonius.[5] One such imaginary speech has survived as the work of Sallust.[6] It is a short, bitter, invective on Cicero's private life, full of historical allusions to the years after Cicero's return from exile, and so well informed that it would seem to have been based on some contemporary political pamphlet, possibly the work of

[1] *ibid. Suas.* 6, 7.
[2] Quint. x. 1, 24.
[3] Sen. *Contr.* iii, *praef.* 15; Quint. x. 5, 20.
[4] Quint. x. 1, 23; 5, 20.
[5] Ascon., p. 93 (Clark).
[6] It has recently been edited by A. Kurfess in the Teubner series. I hold the arguments advanced by Kurfess (in *Mnemosyne* (1912), pp. 364–80) to be decisive against Sallust's authorship. See also Kroll in Teuffel, i, p. 486.

L. Calpurnius Piso.[1] This short invective has a curious history. Dio Cassius gives an imaginary account of a meeting in the senate-house shortly before Cicero's death. Cicero's speech is merely a weak reproduction of his second *Philippic*: [2] but Calenus replies in a long speech, which follows the earlier *Invective* point by point, entering into all the details of Cicero's private life, and distorting every charge into an extravagant caricature.[3] Apparently Dio knew the *Invective* itself, or some later rhetorical amplification of the same theme; and we are thus able to trace the history of this school-declamation for over three centuries.[4]

There is no need to point the contrast between

[1] Schwartz in *Hermes*, vol. xxxiii (1898), p. 106, who quotes Cic. *ad Q. fr.* iii. 1, 11. I do not accept Schwartz's main contention that Piso wrote the *Invective* as we now have it.

[2] Dio, xlv. 18–47; Schwartz in Pauly-Wissowa, iii. 1719.

[3] Dio, xlvi, 1–28; Zielinski, pp. 280 foll.

[4] This is not the place to discuss the interesting problems connected with four 'Pseudo-Sallustiana' to be found in our MSS.; but I should like to say that I regard the two 'Invectives' (*Sallusti in Ciceronem* and *Ciceronis in Sallustium*) as products of the schools of rhetoric: the latter is a typically dull piece of work. The speech *ad Caesarem senem de re publica* is also, I believe, a *suasoria* of some unknown *rhetor*; but its companion-piece, which comes second in our MS., is very probably a genuine political pamphlet written by Sallust in the winter of 50–49 B.C. See Pohlmann's able article in *Sitzb. d. k. bay. Ak. d. Wiss. zu München*, ph.-hist. Kl. (1904), pp. 3–79 [since reprinted in his *Aus Altertum und Gegenwart*, Neue Folge (München, Beck, 1911), pp. 184 foll.]. Pohlmann argues for the authenticity of both pieces; but I cannot agree with him as to the former of the two. Pohlmann's arguments are criticized by Kroll in Teuffel, i, p. 485, and by Schanz (i. 2, p. 185).

these extravagant themes and the historical subjects proposed by Plotius Gallus or by Cicero in his *de Inventione*; still less with the semi-philosophical *theses* which Cicero favoured later in life. Nor was the contrast in any way shunned by the new teachers of rhetoric: on the contrary, they gloried in their extravagances, and deliberately encouraged their pupils to imitate their most obvious faults. Suetonius notes one characteristic innovation. 'The older type of *controversiae*', he says, 'were taken from history, as is occasionally done to-day, or from some true story which might have happened recently; that is why place-names were always added in the plot.'[1] But the new-fangled *controversia* was made as vague and unreal as possible. Place-names were almost always omitted; imaginary pirates and villains, as well as the impossible hero and heroine of a modern film-drama, were the usual stock-in-trade; and the laws which are frequently quoted at the beginning of a plot, and which form the basis of the whole argument proposed for discussion, are taken from an imaginary legal code—partly Greek, partly Roman in its details—which had been gradually elaborated in these schools of rhetoric.[2]

The aim of all this unreality and vagueness was to leave free scope for the professor's imagination. Only the bare minimum of fact was supplied him in the plot. The rest—laws, conventions, locality, secondary personages, scenery and so forth—he was

[1] Suet. *Rhet.* 1.

[2] Bornecque, pp. 59 foll.; Sprenger, *passim*.

free to invent, and these additions to the traditional plot were known as *colores*: a new *color* was as loudly applauded as a brilliant *sententia*. The result was inevitable. No serious argument was possible on such fantastic themes, and declamation became a mere competition in extravagance. The Greek and Latin schools of rhetoric under the Empire helped to create a new literary form, the romance.[1] Their influence on Roman education was wholly disastrous.

The contrast between this new type of rhetoric and the declamations which Cicero knew is marked by a change in the terminology of the schools, which the elder Seneca describes as follows:

> 'Cicero never declaimed what we call *controversiae*, not even those which were in use before his time and which were called *theses*. For this new type of plot which we use in our exercises is so recent that its very name is new. We speak of *controversiae*; Cicero called them *causae*. Another word which we use, *scholastica*—properly a Greek word, but it has become established as a Latin word—is much more recent than *controversia*; just as the word *declamatio* is found in no author earlier than Cicero or Calvus. Calvus defines the meaning of *declamatio* as follows: "To declaim is to speak in private with more than ordinary care." He is right in considering declamation a private exercise, different from true oratory. The word is quite new, just as the fashion itself is of recent origin.'[2]

This attempt at technical lexicography is instructive: but it needs to be checked by actual facts. Seneca is right in his main contention that the terminology of the schools had changed since Cicero's day. But his dogmatic statements lay down a hard and fast rule where none existed, and more than one

[1] Rohde, pp. 361 foll.

[2] Sen. *Contr.* i, *praef.* 12.

modern scholar has allowed them to lead him astray.[1] *Declamatio*, for example, was not first used by Cicero : it is found in the *ad Herennium*,[2] and there is no reason for thinking that the anonymous author invented the word or used it for the first time in its familiar sense of a school-declamation. And Seneca is wrong in his statement that Cicero spoke of *causae*, not *theses* or *controversiae*. Cicero was faced with the problem of translating Greek terminology into Latin, and the Greeks regularly used the terms θέσις and ὑπόθεσις for the two main types of declamation.[3] The Latin words *causa* and *controversia* might be used to translate either of these words, and Cicero's usage varies. In his *de Inventione*, *controversia* means any subject for declamation, whilst ὑπόθεσις is translated by *causa* and θέσις by *quaestio*.[4] In his *de Oratore* both *causa* and *controversia* are used for ὑπόθεσις, whilst θέσις is translated by *quaestio*.[5] And in his latest works ὑπόθεσις is translated by *causa*, θέσις by *propositum*.[6]

It follows that Cicero declaimed both *theses* and *controversiae* : he even prided himself on his interest in the former.[7] Yet for practical purposes Seneca is right in saying that both *controversia* and *declamatio* are new words, for their meaning is now fixed for the

[1] Boissier, *Tacite*, p. 205 ; Wilkins, p. 84 ; Bornecque, pp. 39–48. These scholars wrote before the full evidence was brought together in the *Thesaurus Linguae Latinae* (iii. 689 ; iv. 783).

[2] *ad Her*. iii. 20.

[3] See above, p. 116.

[4] *de Inv*. i. 8, 16 ; ii. 11, 16.

[5] *de Or*. ii. 65 ; iii. 109.

[6] *Part. or*. 61 ; *Top*. 78.

[7] See above, p. 117.

first time, and that meaning is new. *Declamatio* is now the regular word for any school-exercise, whilst *controversia* is used for the imaginary law-suits which had become so popular in the schools of rhetoric. Imaginary deliberations on some more general topic, roughly corresponding to the θέσεις of Hermagoras, are now called *suasoriae*: Cicero occasionally called them *suasiones*.[1] And this terminology remains fixed for a considerable period. Quintilian and Tacitus both speak regularly of *controversiae* and *suasoriae*.[2]

The last word mentioned by Seneca, *scholastica*, has a more significant history. Quintilian occasionally uses it in the sense given by Seneca;[3] but *scholasticus* is more commonly used to denote either a student or professor of rhetoric.[4] The word, with its Greek derivation, emphasizes the growing separation between the new rhetoric of the schools and the old traditions of Roman oratory. Cicero would have called the new style an *umbratilis doctrina*, with the true orator's contempt for an art that was afraid of the open air and the forum;[5] and Pliny actually couples the two words *scholasticus* and *umbraticus*.[6]

One of these 'indoor orators' is caricatured by Petronius in his *Satire*;[7] but the stories told by the elder Seneca of the *rhetores* whom he knew in actual

[1] *de Or.* ii. 333; *Or.* 37. [2] Quint. *passim*; Tac. *Dial.* 14.

[3] Quint. vii. 1, 14; xi. 1, 82.

[4] Sen. *Contr.* iii, *praef.* 16; Petron. *Sat.* 6, 10; Pliny, *Epp.* ii. 3, 5; Tac. *Dial.* 15, 42.

[5] *de Or.* i. 157; *Or.* 64. [6] Plin. *Epp.* ix. 2, 3.

[7] Petron. *Sat.* 2.

life are so fantastic that they defy the caricaturist. Porcius Latro is as good a specimen as any. According to Seneca, who came from the same town as Latro and knew him well, this Spanish schoolmaster was the greatest declaimer of his day. His talent for extemporary oratory was amazing, his physique powerful enough to stand the strain of his impassioned delivery, and his memory unfailingly retentive: 'no man had greater control of his talent, and no man abused it more frequently'.[1] Yet Latro was helpless when called upon to address any audience outside his class-room. On one occasion he was asked to speak in the forum on behalf of a kinsman. The unfamiliar surroundings were too much for him: he began with a blunder in grammar, broke down, and was unable to continue until the magistrate, out of respect for the distinguished orator, transferred the court from the open air to a neighbouring basilica.[2]

Even more quaint are the stories told by Seneca of another *rhetor*, Cestius Pius. Cestius was a Greek by birth, but had made his fame as a teacher of Latin rhetoric.[3] Seneca does not include him in his 'tetrad' of great declaimers, Porcius Latro, Arellius Fuscus, Albucius Silo, and Junius Gallio,[4] but the omission is probably due to personal prejudice. For Cestius was a leader of the anti-Ciceronian party, whilst Seneca

[1] Sen. *Contr.* i, *praef.* 13–24.
[2] *ibid.* ix, *praef.* 3; Quint. x. 5, 18.
[3] Sen. *Contr.* ix. 3, 13; Bornecque, p. 160.
[4] Sen. *Contr.* x, *praef.* 13.

held that Roman oratory died with Cicero.[1] Cestius pushed his contempt for Cicero to extremes. 'He was an ignorant fellow', the *rhetor* would tell his pupils; and they took his word for it, skimming through Cicero's speeches whilst they learnt by heart the declamations which Cestius wrote in answer to the orator.[2] The pose did not go unpunished: for Cicero's drunken young son, Marcus, once ordered Cestius to be whipped by his slaves at a dinner in his house.[3] But Cicero's honour was more worthily avenged by Cassius Severus, a leading orator of the Augustan age whom Tacitus mentions as one of the first to use the new style of rhetoric in his oratory.[4] Cassius was one day present at a lecture given by Cestius, when the *rhetor* began to brag about his success. 'If I were a gladiator', he said, 'I would be Fusius; if I were a dancer, I would be Bathyllus; if I were a racehorse, I would be Melissio.' The allusions were to favourites of the day: but the retort was unexpected. 'Yes,' cried Cassius from the back of the hall,[3] 'and if you were a town-drain, you would be the *cloaca maxima*.'[5] And on another occasion Cassius exposed the *rhetor's* helplessness by dragging him from one court in the forum to another; accusing him first of felony, then of ingratitude, then of madness, because he thought himself more eloquent than Cicero. Poor Cestius was

[1] Sen. *Contr.* i, *praef.* 6.
[2] *ibid.* iii, *praef.* 15; ix. 3, 12; Quint. x. 5, 20.
[3] Sen. *Suas.* 7, 13.
[4] Tac. *Dial.* 19.
[5] Sen. *Contr.* iii, *praef.* 16 (Cassius is being quoted by Seneca).

unable to silence his persecutor, and at last had to be forcibly rescued by his friends.[1]

A story like that brings home the point of a criticism made by the younger Seneca in one of his *Letters to Lucilius*: 'We educate ourselves for the class-room, not for life: hence the extravagances with which we are troubled, in literature as in everything else.'[2] Yet these new schools of rhetoric, with all their artificial brilliance and 'indoor oratory', were patronized by the leaders of Augustan culture. Augustus himself was a frequent visitor at the public declamations given in the schools, and he was sometimes accompanied by Tiberius.[3] Maecenas, whose own literary style was modelled on the new rhetoric,[4] Messalla, Agrippa, and Asinius Pollio are all mentioned by the elder Seneca as regular visitors.[5] Pollio's criticisms were considered authoritative, and he even declaimed himself before a carefully selected audience.[6] And Suetonius tells us that the fashion for declamation increased steadily under the reign of Tiberius, reaching its height under Nero, who was himself a keen student of rhetoric.[7]

But the most characteristic figure in all this literary history is Ovid, the poet whose verses were the model for declaimers as well as for poets,[8] and

[1] *ibid.* iii, *praef.* 17. [2] Sen. *Epp.* 106, 12.
[3] Sen. *Contr.* ii. 4, 12–13; iv, *praef.* 7; x. 5, 21; *Suas.* 3, 6–7.
[4] Suet. *Oct.* 86; Sen. *Epp.* 114, 4–8; Quint. ix. 4, 28; Tac. *Dial.* 26. [5] Sen. *Contr.* ii. 4, 12; *Suas.* 3, 6.
[6] Sen. *Contr.* iv, *praef.* 2–5; Bornecque, p. 155.
[7] Suet. *Rhet.* 1; *Nero*, 10.
[8] Sen. *Contr.* iii., Exc. 7; ix. 5, 17; x. 4, 25; Vergil was also

whose rhetoric was as elegant as his verse. Ovid tells us himself that his father had made him study rhetoric under the best professors in Rome,[1] and Seneca mentions Latro, Gallio, and Arellius Fuscus as his masters.[2] Here is Seneca's description of the poet's performance, sketched from life :

'His style was elegant, appropriate and agreeable ; even then his oratory was unmistakably poetry in prose. He was so keen a student of Latro's declamations that he inserted many of Latro's *sententiae* in his poems. He rarely declaimed *controversiae,* and only when the subject had some psychological interest : his preference was for *suasoriae.* All argument was distasteful to him. His choice of words was never extravagant, except in his poems : there he knew his fault, but loved it.' [3]

That last phrase might be applied to all these *rhetores*. Cestius Pius, for example, once made the following frank admission to his class : ' Here I know that I am talking nonsense ; but I say many things to please my audience, not to please myself.' [4] And another *rhetor*, Votienus Montanus, was even more frank in a private conversation with the elder Seneca. ' A man who composes a declamation ', he said, ' does not write to convince, but to please. That is why he seeks out tricks of style, and leaves argument alone, because it is troublesome and gives little scope for rhetoric. He is content to beguile his audience with his *sententiae* and digressions :

much admired by the *rhetores* (Sen. *Suas.* 3, 4–7 ; Comparetti, pp. 34 foll.).

[1] Ovid. *Trist.* iv. 10, 15.

[2] Sen. *Contr.* ii. 2, 8 ; *Suas.* 3, 7.

[3] Sen. *Contr.* ii. 2, 8–12.

[4] *ibid.* ix. 6, 12.

for he wants to be applauded, not to win his case.'[1]

The transition from oratory to rhetoric could hardly be expressed more plainly, and the unreality of these new declamations was not confined to their artificial and exaggerated style. Legal argument and historical truth were both neglected by the *rhetores*, the latter to a degree which modern taste would find intolerable. One or two examples may be quoted. Seneca's collection of *Suasoriae* includes one on the three hundred Spartans at Thermopylae: a sufficiently dramatic setting for any lover of rhetoric. But the theme, as he propounds it, shows how even the most familiar story was twisted by the *rhetores* for their purposes. The three hundred Spartans are supported by a battalion of three hundred from every Greek state: all have fled and the Spartan battalion remains alone.[2] And in a *controversia* we learn that the people of Elea ordered the hands of Pheidias to be cut off for sacrilege![3] Tacitus complains that history was neglected in the schools of rhetoric.[4] His complaint is borne out by the elder Seneca, who apologizes to his sons for an historical digression which he makes towards the end of his *Suasoriae*. They prefer rhetoric to history, he knows; so he adds one last *suasoria* to his collection, for fear they should stop reading where he has deserted the *scholastici*.[5]

[1] *ibid*. ix, *praef*. 1.
[2] Sen. *Suas*. 2; Bornecque, pp. 86 foll.
[3] Sen. *Contr*. viii. 2.
[4] Tac. *Dial*. 29.
[5] Sen. *Suas*. 6, 16, 27.

But what of the *exempla* from Roman history which Cicero and Quintilian both recommend to their students ? How could they be aptly used without a thorough knowledge of Greek and Roman history ? Roman publishers asked themselves the question, and the demand was not long in producing the supply. The *Memorable Sayings and Doings* of Valerius Maximus is a book which few students of Latin literature take the trouble to read ; and they do well. But the book is important in the history of Roman education ; for it was written to save students of rhetoric the labour of studying Greek and Roman history. Valerius Maximus makes this quite plain in his preface. He has written the book, he tells us, 'to spare those who want to learn the lessons of history the trouble of prolonged researches ' ; [1] and this politely vague formula indicates the teachers and students of rhetoric. The book is planned exactly according to their needs, and is best described as a dictionary of rhetorical *exempla*. No attempt is made at chronological order or connected narrative. Each incident is an isolated episode, designed to illustrate a particular virtue or vice, and grouped under some convenient heading. The first book, for example, treats of religion, and is subdivided into chapters on superstition, omens, prodigies, dreams, and miracles. The second book treats of various national institutions ; the third of human character, and is subdivided into chapters on fortitude, patience, and so forth. As a manual for use in

[1] Val. Max. *praef.* 1 ; Norden, i, p. 303.

schools of rhetoric, the work is admirably planned: as a text-book of Roman history it is a tell-tale document. Cicero had very different ideas when he bade his orator study Roman history for its lessons of wisdom and virtue.

The elder Seneca spent most of his life in the schools of rhetoric, and only wearied of the art in his old age.[1] But his judgement on the value of these artificial performances is sound, and may be taken as summing up the tendencies described in this and the preceding chapter. Addressing his three sons in the preface to his *Controversiae* he says:

> 'You are right, my boys, not to be contented with the models of your own generation, but to want to hear about earlier days. The more models you study, the greater will be your progress in oratory. And you will learn also to judge the decline which has set in and the decadence into which, by some perversion of nature, our oratory has fallen. For all the great Roman orators who can be compared with the glories of Greece, or even preferred to them, lived in the days of Cicero: all the men of genius who have shed lustre on our schools were born in that generation. Since then things have gone from bad to worse: partly because of our increasing luxury, for luxury is always fatal to genius partly because there is no prize left for the noblest of arts, and all our energies are given to the vices which now win honour and wealth; partly because nature's stern law requires that all high achievement shall end in a fall, swifter than our ascent to the heights.'[2]

§ 3. *Rhetoric and Philosophy.*

'By a perversion of nature', to use Seneca's own phrase, one of the boys to whom these words were addressed was to become the greatest personal

[1] Sen. *Contr.* x, *praef.* 1; *Suas.* 2, 23; 6, 16.
[2] Sen. *Contr.* i, *praef.* 6–7.

factor in the reaction against Ciceronian ideals. The younger Seneca's life presents a curiously close parallelism with Cicero's personal history. Both were *novi homines*, who owed their social position to their talent and the charm of their personality ; both were students rather than men of action, by temperament literary artists, not statesmen or politicians. Yet both were called upon to take a leading part in contemporary politics ; and both died—not ignobly—the victims of their political failure. Both men, too, felt the fascination of Greek philosophy, and gave much of their energies to popularizing Greek thought in Rome ; and both showed an amazingly varied facility of production. But there the likeness ends. Cicero was an orator who found in philosophy the means of satisfying his intellectual curiosity ; Seneca was a philosopher, suspicious of everything that might distract him from his habits of introspection and his interest in moral principles. Yet the *Letters to Lucilius* are as typical of their age as are the *de Oratore* and the *Hortensius*.

For philosophy, like rhetoric, had changed its character under the stress of a social revolution. Just as Caesar's dictatorship forced Cicero to question the ethical foundations on which his philosophy rested and led him to write the *Hortensius*, the *Tusculan Disputations*, and the *de Officiis*, so the permanent establishment of the Empire under Augustus and his immediate successors forced thoughtful men back upon themselves and gave their philosophy a new purpose. Two figures are prominent in the history of Roman philosophy between Cicero and Seneca: Q. Sextius, the founder of a new school, half Stoic, half Pythagorean in its tenets,[1] and L. Annaeus Cornutus, a Stoic and the tutor of Persius and Lucan.[2] Both men were primarily interested in questions of moral conduct, and both show that marked tendency to an austere self-denial which is henceforth characteristic of Roman Stoicism. It was just this ethical austerity that gave these men their influence: for the first time in the history of Roman society we hear of 'conversions' to philosophy involving a radical change in the convert's manner of life. One of the earliest is described by Suetonius.[3] L. Crassicius, a native of Tarentum but of Latin rather than Greek culture, began life as a playwright and then opened a school of Latin literature. The school proved a success and became fashionable; but just as Crassicius was beginning to rival Verrius Flaccus, then at the height of his fame, he came under the influence of Sextius, closed his school and joined the new philosophical sect. Similarly Papirius Fabianus, a brilliant young *rhetor* who had studied rhetoric under Arellius Fuscus, and was making a name for himself at a very early age, suddenly threw up rhetoric for philosophy and joined the school of Sextius.[4] His conversion is of peculiar interest,

[1] Sen. *Epp.* 59, 7; 64, 2–5; Hirzel in Gardthausen, iii. 1, pp. 1296 foll.

[2] *Vit. Pers.* 4; *Vit. Lucan.*; Schanz, i, 2, pp. 372 foll.

[3] Suet. *Gram.* 18.

[4] Sen. *Contr.* ii, *praef.* 1–2; Bornecque, p. 185.

because it involved a break with his former literary style. As a *rhetor* Fabianus had indulged in every extravagance of the new manner: as a philosopher he continued his study of rhetoric, but aimed at a simpler style and achieved real eloquence, so we are told, in spite of occasional obscurity.[1]

A generation later Persius went through a similar intellectual crisis at the age of sixteen: from being a pupil of Remmius Palaemon and a keen student of rhetoric he became the disciple of Annaeus Cornutus and gave himself wholly to the study of Stoic philosophy.[2] But the most famous of all these youthful conversions is described by Seneca in his *Letters to Lucilius*.[3] The philosopher's father had set his heart on seeing his three sons become great orators. The eldest, Novatus, was adopted by the *rhetor* Junius Gallio, and figures as the proconsul Gallio in the Acts of the Apostles. The youngest, Mela, became a professor of rhetoric himself and was the father of Lucan. Seneca himself was the favourite son, and was urged by his father to become an advocate. But his real taste was for philosophy, which he had studied under Fabianus, Attalus, and Sotion, all of them philosophers of the new austere type.[4] A struggle was inevitable, for his father disliked philosophy, and had already prevented Seneca's mother Helvia from interesting herself in it.[5]

[1] Sen. *Contr.* ii, *praef.* 5; Sen. *Epp.* 100. [2] *Vit. Pers.* 4–5.
[3] Sen. *Epp.* 108, 13–22; Waltz, pp. 31 foll.
[4] Sen. *Epp.* 49, 2; 52, 11; 100, 12; 108, 3.
[5] Sen. *ad Helv. matr.* 17, 4.

The crisis came when Seneca began to adopt a vegetarian diet. He had already learnt to live poorly, to drink no wine, to sleep on a hard couch, to refuse oysters and mushrooms at table and so forth: this last extravagance was too much. The boy's health was beginning to suffer, and his father insisted on a more normal diet. Seneca yielded, but the change was only external. As an old man he boasts that, whatever else might be said of him, he had always been faithful to his hard couch:[1] no bad test of practical Stoicism.

Seneca was not the only young man of his time to make these experiments in diet, and the change from Cicero's ideal of philosophy is evident. The days were past when an orator could plunge into the study of philosophy and yet lose none of his interest in rhetoric. Under the Empire philosophy becomes a definite profession, involving definite moral obligations and separating the philosopher, even in externals, from the ordinary life of Rome: an isolation which makes philosophy more than ever suspect in the eyes of Roman conservatives as well as the imperial government. And this isolation tended to force philosophy out of the ordinary 'encyclic' programme of studies: for the *ἐγκύκλιος παιδεία* was by its very name an education for the ordinary man. One of Seneca's *Letters to Lucilius* makes the point clear. Posidonius had divided the 'arts' into two classes: the truly 'liberal' arts, which teach virtue and nothing else, and the 'childish'

[1] Sen. *Epp.* 108, 23.

arts (*pueriles*), 'which the Greeks call ἐγκύκλιοι and the Romans *liberales*'.[1] Seneca approves of the distinction, and justifies it in an elaborate criticism of all the *artes liberales.* One by one they are analysed in turn and shown to be incapable of teaching moral excellence. 'Are they of any use?' Seneca asks himself, and the answer is characteristic of his attitude: 'They are useful for everything else, but not for virtue. Like the manual arts which are admittedly vulgar, they are of great practical utility, but have no relation to virtue. Then why do we teach our children the liberal arts? Not because they can give virtue, but because they prepare the mind to receive virtue.'[2] Or as he had already put it in a characteristic epigram: 'Our duty is not to study them, but to have studied them.'[3]

Plainly this ideal of a philosophic life differs widely from Cicero's *politior humanitas,* and it is no mere accident that this very letter from Seneca to Lucilius contains a definition of *humanitas* which limits that virtue to the practice of kindliness and natural affection.[4] Seneca's definition lacks Cicero's intellectual breadth of view, and his more narrow ideal of human excellence marks a falling-off from the earlier Graeco-Roman ideal. But it would be wrong to take Seneca's attack on the *artes liberales* too seriously. In an essay *On Consolation,* written when he was in exile and dedicated to his mother, he bids her take refuge from her grief in the study of the

[1] Sen. *Epp.* 88, 21–3. [2] *ibid.* 88, 20. [3] *ibid.* 88, 2.
[4] *ibid.* 88, 30; cf. *Epp.* 4, 10; 81, 26; 116, 5.

liberal arts: 'They will heal your wound, they will pluck care from your heart, as they do for all who fly to them from misfortune.'[1] And even in the letter to Lucilius on the *artes liberales* there is one notable omission. Literature, music, geometry, arithmetic, astronomy, painting, sculpture, athletics: all these are examined in turn, and rejected. Not a word is said about rhetoric. Elsewhere Seneca definitely ranks eloquence as beneath philosophy,[2] but here rhetoric, the most conspicuous of all the *artes*, is passed by in silence. Possibly Seneca did not wish to condemn in public an art which had made his brothers famous: or was there a more personal motive? No writer of the period is more rhetorical than this austere moralist: Seneca declaiming against rhetoric might have made even Lucilius smile.

[1] Sen. *ad Helv. matr.* 17, 3.

[2] Sen. *Epp.* 40, 12.

IX

QUINTILIAN

Quintiliane, vagae moderator summe iuventae,
Gloria, Romanae, Quintiliane, togae. Mart. ii. 90.

§ 1. *The 'Institutio Oratoria'.*

QUINTILIAN was a Spaniard and a professional man, who owed his fortune wholly to the Empire. No better type of the new society could be desired, and the *Institutio Oratoria* should be read in the light of its author's antecedents. For Quintilian is a Ciceronian; but his Ciceronianism is something new and personal, the product partly of his own study and enthusiasm, partly of his surroundings.

According to Ausonius and St. Jerome,[1] who are both most probably dependent for their information on a lost chapter of the *de Claris rhetoribus*,[2] Quintilian was a native of Calagurris in Northern Spain (Tarraconensis). Of his early life we know nothing, though his birth must be dated somewhere between A.D. 30 and 40.[3] As a young man (*adulescentulus*) he was in Rome and an admirer of Domitius Afer, the famous orator from Nemausus in Gallia Narbonensis.[4]

[1] Auson. *prof. Burd.* 1, 7; St. Jerome, *Chron.*, A.D. 88.

[2] See the index to the lost chapters in Reifferscheid's text, p. 99.

[3] Schanz, ii. 2, p. 453; Colson, p. ix.

[4] Quint. v. 7, 7; vi. 1, 14; x. 1, 86; xii. 11, 3.

Possibly Quintilian had gone from Calagurris to Rome as a school-boy : at any rate he was a student of rhetoric there before A.D. 58, the date of Afer's death. An unknown scholiast on Juvenal's sixth satire names Quintilian as a pupil of Remmius Palaemon,[1] and there is nothing in the chronology to make us doubt this statement ; but Quintilian himself, who quotes Palaemon,[2] does not speak of him as his master, and it is possible that the scholiast is wrong. Once his studies were completed, Quintilian went back to Spain, probably as an advocate as well as a teacher of rhetoric. The combination of the two professions was not unusual,[3] and Quintilian practised them both later in life at Rome.[4]

Quintilian returned to Rome in A.D. 68 as a client of the Emperor Galba,[5] and remained there for the rest of his life. Galba was murdered a few months after his arrival, but Quintilian soon found a more powerful patron. Vespasian, the self-made Emperor, took an interest in the successful schoolmaster, and made him the first public professor of Latin rhetoric in Rome. The appointment marks a definite stage in the history of Roman educational policy, and needs a word of explanation. Our information is derived ultimately from Suetonius, but the most important detail has got confused by St. Jerome in his *Chronicle* for the year A.D. 88.

[1] Schol. ad Juv. vi. 452. [2] Quint. i. 4, 20 ; Colson, p. x.
[3] Mart. ii. 64 ; Friedlaender, i, p. 180 (i, p. 328).
[4] Quint. iv. 2, 86 ; vii. 2, 5 ; 2, 24 ; ix. 2, 73.
[5] St. Jerome, *Chron.*, A.D. 68.

Suetonius tells us that Vespasian 'was the first to establish a fixed salary (100,000 sesterces a year) for teachers of Latin and Greek rhetoric'.[1] The words are vague, and might mean a general subsidy for distinguished professors; but we can supplement this statement from another source. In his *Lives of the Sophists* Philostratus frequently mentions a public chair of Greek rhetoric at Rome,[2] and distinguishes it from a similar chair which the Emperor Hadrian had founded at Athens, by the title of 'the upper chair' (ὁ ἄνω θρόνος).[3] This is plainly the kind of chair to which St. Jerome alludes in his entry for the year A. D. 88: 'Quintilian, a native of Calagurris in Spain, was the first to get a public chair (*publicam scholam*) at Rome and a salary from the fiscus, and was famous.'[4] The fiscus was the imperial treasury, and Vespasian's endowment was an imperial act: so that our authorities confirm one another on this point. Furthermore a salary of 100,000 sesterces had been paid by Augustus to Verrius Flaccus as the tutor of his two grandsons,[5] and was equivalent to a post in the second division of the imperial civil service.[6]

One difficulty remains: Vespasian died in A. D. 79, and St. Jerome dates the entry in his *Chronicle* to

[1] Suet. *Vesp.* 18.

[2] Philost. *Vit. Soph.* (ed. Kayser), 580, 589, 594, 596, 627.

[3] *ibid.* 623.

[4] There is no need to change the wording of St. Jerome's text, as has been done by modern critics without any manuscript authority.

[5] Suet. *Gram.* 17.

[6] Barbagallo, p. 89.

A.D. 88. The conflict of authority is only apparent, for St. Jerome has borrowed a whole series of entries about distinguished orators and teachers from Suetonius,[1] and there is no reason to think that this entry about Quintilian is taken from any other source. But St. Jerome is notoriously inaccurate, and his *Chronicle* was put together in a hurry. The date which he gives must be wrong, and Quintilian's appointment must fall between the years A.D. 70 and 79. The opening words of the *Institutio Oratoria* suggest a date somewhere between 70 and 73; for Quintilian there says that he is writing his work 'now that I have been granted a rest from my labours of the past twenty years in the education of youth'. These words are usually understood as referring to his whole career as teacher, both in Spain and at Rome; but they plainly allude to his position as public professor in the imperial service: otherwise there would be no sense in talking of a rest which had been granted him by somebody (*post impetratam studiis meis quietem*). Now there is excellent reason for dating the first book of the *Institutio Oratoria* between A.D. 91 and 93,[2] and Quintilian speaks of his retirement as 'some time ago' (*iam pridem*) in the second book.[3] It follows that the appointment should probably be dated some twenty years earlier, about A.D. 71.

[1] St. Jerome, *Chron.*, 88 B.C. (= Suet. *Rhet.* 2); 81 B.C. (= *ibid.* 3); 6 B.C. (= *ibid.* 6); 9 B.C. (= Suet. *Gram.* 20); 4 B.C. (= *ibid.* 21). The question has been studied by Mommsen in his *Quellen der Chronik des Hieronymus.*

[2] Schanz, ii. 2, p. 457.

[3] Quint. ii. 12, 12.

Quintilian's position as public professor of Latin rhetoric marked him out as the head of his profession, and all the allusions to his name in the literature of the period show that Quintilian was a man of high social standing. Juvenal, who was himself a teacher of rhetoric and knew the seamy side of his profession, cites Quintilian as the one conspicuous exception to his general complaint that schoolmasters are ill-paid and over-worked;[1] Martial addresses flattering verses to his distinguished compatriot;[2] and Pliny is obviously proud of the fact that Quintilian was his master.[3] Fortune follows the fortunate, and Quintilian's record as public professor earned him towards the end of his life a second appointment as tutor to the two sons of Flavius Clemens.[4] The boys had just been adopted by Domitian as heirs to his throne, and the appointment seems to have carried with it the consular *insignia*: an honour which Quintilian owed, so Ausonius tells us, to the influence of Flavius Clemens.[5] From first to last Quintilian's record is thus the type of a successful career; and his educational theory represents the experience of a highly-favoured and fashionable professor, not of an ordinary Roman schoolmaster. Many of the counsels given in the *Institutio Oratoria* need to be read in the light of these facts.

The *Institutio Oratoria* was written some time after Quintilian's retirement. Two years were needed to

[1] Juv. vi. 75, 280; vii. 186 foll.
[2] Mart. ii. 90.
[3] Pliny, *Epp.* ii. 14, 10; vi. 6, 3.
[4] Quint. iv, *prooem.* 2.
[5] Auson. *Grat. act.* 7, 31.

complete it,[1] and the date of publication should probably be fixed between A.D. 93 and 95. It was not Quintilian's first attempt at literary work. As a young man he had published a speech (*actio*) for which he apologizes in his old age; [2] and three years or so before he began work on the *Institutio* he published an essay *On the Decay of Oratory and its Causes*,[3] which must have covered some of the ground later gone over more thoroughly in the longer work. For the *Institutio oratoria* is more than a text-book of rhetoric. Its very title marks it off as something distinct from the ordinary manual (*Ars rhetorica*, or *de Arte dicendi*).[4] Quintilian himself mentions the title of his work in his prefatory letter to the book-seller Trypho,[5] and explains in his preface to the first book why he chose this unusual form.

'All others who have written on the art of oratory begin by presupposing an ordinary general education, and assume that their task is to give the finishing touch of eloquence.[6] Perhaps they despised the preparatory studies as less important; or perhaps they considered them to be outside their proper work, now that the professions are divided; or, most probably, they saw no prospect of popularity for good work on a subject which is very necessary, but unostentatious: men usually admire the roof of a building, and forget the foundations. In my opinion, nothing that is necessary for the training of an orator is foreign

[1] Quint. *praef. ad Tryph.* 1.
[2] *ibid.* vii. 2, 24.
[3] *ibid.* vi, *prooem.* 3; Schanz, ii. 2, p. 454.
[4] Quint. ii. 17, 2; Börner, pp. 11 foll.
[5] *Institutio Oratoria* is the title given in the best manuscript; the others are divided between *Institutiones oratoriae* and *de Institutione oratoria* (Schanz, ii. 2, p. 457).
[6] See Colson's note *ad loc.*

to the art of oratory: you never can get to the top without beginning somewhere. Therefore, I shall not disdain those less important subjects without which the more important have no place, but shall begin my orator's education just as though he had been given me to bring up from infancy.'[1]

'The Education of an Orator' would thus be the most accurate translation of Quintilian's title.[2] But what did Quintilian mean by an orator? Here again the answer can be given in his own words:

'The orator whom we are educating is the perfect orator, who can only be a good man: and therefore we demand of him, not merely an excellent power of speech, but all the moral virtues as well. Nor am I prepared to admit (as some have held) that the science of a righteous and honourable life should be left to the philosophers: for the man who is a true citizen, fit for the administration of private and public business, and capable of guiding cities by his counsels, establishing them by his laws and reforming them by his judgements, is none other than the orator.'[3]

There is no need to ask where Quintilian got this ideal of the 'perfect orator'. Every page of the *Institutio oratoria* is reminiscent of Cicero's teaching, but here the borrowing is more than usually evident. Quintilian has gone back to the *de Oratore* for his definition, and the 'perfect orator' whose education he describes is none other than the *doctus orator* of Cicero's dialogue.[4] Nor does Quintilian make any attempt to conceal his indebtedness. The *de Oratore* is expressly quoted a few lines further on,[5] and the

[1] Quint. i, *prooem.* 4–5.

[2] Börner, p. 17, who analyses Quintilian's use of the words *instituere* and *institutio*.

[3] Quint. i, *prooem.* 9–10.

[4] See above, p. 112.

[5] Quint. i, *prooem.* 13.

Ciceronian character of his teaching is never for a moment in doubt. His list of the authors, Greek and Latin, who had written before him on the art of rhetoric, contains the following noteworthy sentence:

'M. Tullius, our one incomparable model of oratory and oratorical theory, has shed most light on the rules of eloquence as well as on eloquence itself. Modesty would keep me silent after his work, did he not himself say that he had let fall his text-book of rhetoric [the *de Inventione*] as a mere boy; moreover, he has deliberately omitted those less important subjects which are usually missing in our text-books.' [1]

Quintilian's ideal is thus a conscious return to the teaching of the *de Oratore* and the *Orator*; and the title *Institutio oratoria* implies a challenge to contemporary thought. For the words 'orator' and 'oratory' had shifted their meaning since the days of Cicero, and Quintilian's contemporaries were aware of the fact. Tacitus, for example, notes the change in his *Dialogue on Orators*: 'Our generation is barren of orators. We have lost the glory of eloquence and we have barely kept the name of orator. For we use the word only when speaking of the ancients: our modern speakers we call pleaders (*causidici*) or advocates (*advocati*) or barristers (*patroni*) or anything but orators.' [2] Quintilian himself recognizes this distinction between *orator* and *causidicus*; for in his twelfth book he contrasts his own ideal of oratory with the 'hired eloquence' of a mere pleader—'a *causidicus*, to use the vulgar phrase'.[3] And a similar distinction is to be noted

[1] *ibid.* iii. 1, 20; there is a similar acknowledgement in ix. 4, 1.
[2] Tac. *Dial.* 1. [3] Quint. xii. 1, 25.

between his use of the words *rhetoricus* and *oratorius*. Cicero's great dialogues on oratory—the *de Oratore*, *Orator*, and *Brutus*—are described as *libri oratorii*; but the two books of the *de Inventione*, a mere text-book of rhetoric, are called *libri rhetorici*.[1]

In the light of these facts it is interesting to note how frequently Quintilian uses the word *orator* and its cognate forms in the opening pages of his *Institutio*. His pupils, he says, had asked him to write a treatise on rhetoric; and their suggestion is described in a conventional phrase (*ut aliquid de ratione dicendi componerem*).[2] But once Quintilian begins to speak of his own purpose his language alters. *Ars orandi*, *ars oratoria*, *orator*, *orator perfectus*: the very words have a stately sound, and the frequency with which they recur[3] shows that Quintilian is consciously recalling Ciceronian memories. To his readers the whole preface must have sounded like a direct challenge. Political oratory was dead, and every one in Rome knew that it was dead; but Quintilian deliberately chooses the oratory of a past generation as his educational ideal.

The whole structure of Quintilian's work illustrates the significance of its title. Of the twelve books into which it is divided, only nine, so Quintilian tells us himself,[4] would usually be included in a text-book of rhetoric. Book I deals with the education of a boy before he begins the study of rhetoric. Book II gives general advice about the studies which are proper to

[1] Quint. iii. 1, 20.
[2] *ibid.* i, *prooem.* 1.
[3] *ibid.* i, *prooem.* 4–6, 9–10.
[4] *ibid.* ii. 11, 1; iii. 1, 1.

the school of rhetoric, and discusses the nature of rhetoric as a science. The theory of rhetoric proper begins only in Book III, and is continued—with a famous digression in Book X—to the end of Book XI. Book XII gives advice to the orator who has left school, and wishes to carry his art to perfection in the ordinary work of his profession; and Quintilian inserts here his theory of the higher studies which should be made after leaving the school of rhetoric. This division of his subject-matter implies a contrast with the *de Oratore* as well as with the contemporary text-books of rhetoric. In Cicero's phraseology, only portions of Books X and XII deal with the *politior humanitas.* By far the largest part of Quintilian's work is concerned with the ordinary *puerilis institutio*; and this difference of proportion is significant. Cicero was a man of the world and a great orator, writing for men of his own kind. Quintilian was a successful and experienced schoolmaster, accustomed to think in terms of the classroom: that is why he gives us our best insight into the practical work of Graeco-Roman education.

§ 2. *Preliminary Studies.*

True to his promise, Quintilian begins his theory of education with the child's first lessons; and it is plain from the outset that he is writing for the children of the rich. Not a word is said about the elementary schoolmaster (*ludi magister*) and his classes. The children who came to Quintilian's school had got their first lessons at home, and his advice concerns the choice of a nurse, the need of proper companions for the boy, and the duties of the *paedagogus* (who was a sort of companion and mentor, frequently also a tutor). The main point is that they should be honest, reliable folk, with good accents ;[1] the *paedagogus* is not to be allowed to teach the child unless he is unusually well educated.[2] Lessons are to begin as soon as the child can speak, and here Chrysippus is quoted as against Eratosthenes.[3] But the language in which the child speaks raises a difficulty: is it to be Greek or Latin ? Quintilian admits that the child is bound to pick up Latin from those around him, but he wants the first lessons to be given in Greek: 'partly because he will be soaked in Latin whether we like it or not, partly because at school he will have to begin with Greek ; for our whole educational system is derived from Greek.'[4] These first Greek lessons are not to be pushed too far: correct Latin is the primary requirement, and it would be easy to spoil the child's accent and grammar. The rest of the chapter gives minute instructions as to the best way of teaching the alphabet and giving the first lessons in reading and writing, with some very sensible remarks as to the value of good handwriting.[5] Quintilian's practical sense shows itself again at the end of the chapter. Memory-lessons are to be given, but the matter to be memorized should be carefully chosen. Good proverbs and counsels of great men should be learnt by

[1] Quint. i. 1, 4, 7–8. [2] *ibid.* 8. [3] *ibid.* 15–19.
[4] *ibid.* 12 ; see Colson's note. [5] Quint. i. 1, 28.

heart, as well as pieces that will increase the child's vocabulary.[1] And it is no harm to make children learn sentences by heart that are difficult to pronounce quickly: later in life they may easily form habits of careless or faulty pronunciation, which might have been cured by this simple means.[2]

One or two of the details mentioned by Quintilian show plainly that he is writing for the well-to-do: the child's toy-alphabet, for example, is made of ivory,[3] and his suggestion that the lessons should be helped out by prizes reminds us of Verrius Flaccus, who made his school of literature fashionable by a similar system.[4] But the next chapter raises a question which could only be asked by a rich parent. Is it better for a boy to be sent to school or to be taught by a private tutor at home? Quintilian claims all the weight of authority for his own opinion that a boy should always be sent to school.[5] His reasons are mainly from the teacher's point of view: it is easier to be interested in a large class than in private tuition; most subjects can be taught as well to large numbers in a class-room as to a single boy; and competition is the life of a school. On this last point he has an interesting personal reminiscence. His own schoolmasters, whom he leaves unnamed, used to arrange the boys in class according to merit. Regular competitions were held for the privilege of declaiming first in public: the privilege lasted a

[1] *ibid.* 35–6. [2] *ibid.* 37. [3] *ibid.* 26.
[4] *ibid.* 20; Suet. *Gram.* 17.
[5] Quint. i. 2, 2.

month, when the competition was renewed—a device which Quintilian commends.[1]

One of the arguments urged by Quintilian as an objection against school education is of special interest. What about the boy's morals? Will he not be safer at home? Quintilian meets the objection by a somewhat rhetorical attack on parents who spoil their children at home, and on the dangers of companionship with the slaves of the household.[2] His complaints are borne out by other writers of the period: Petronius, the elder Pliny, Seneca, and Tacitus.[3] But the really significant fact is that Quintilian, speaking from experience, freely admits the dangers of school-life. There is, of course, the danger of loose conversation with one's school-fellows,[4] but Quintilian is thinking of a graver evil. What if the master himself should be the cause of trouble? Quintilian was most probably the pupil of Remmius Palaemon: in any case he must have known all the scandal connected with Palaemon's name, and he may well have been thinking of Palaemon when he insists on the need of care in choosing a trustworthy teacher: especially in the later stages of a boy's schooling.[5]

All these early chapters of the *Institutio* make very interesting reading. Quintilian discusses, for example, the age at which a child should be sent to school.

[1] Quint. i. 2, 23–5; see Colson's note. [2] *ibid.* 6–8.

[3] Petron. *Sat.* 4; Pliny, *N. H.* xxxiii. 26–7; Sen. *Epp.* 60, 1; 94, 54; 115, 11; Tac. *Dial.* 28–9.

[4] Quint. i. 2, 4. [5] *ibid.* i. 2, 5; 3, 17; ii. 2, 1–4, 15.

Seven was evidently the usual age for beginning lessons; but Quintilian agrees with Chrysippus that lessons had better begin much earlier, with the nurse as teacher.[1] His own phrase for describing the age at which he would have a boy go to school is vague: 'when he begins to grow up and leave the nursery, and can do serious study'.[2] Any lessons that may have been given before that age should be made as attractive as possible: the child is not yet old enough to enjoy study, but at least he should not learn to hate it.[3] Similarly Quintilian has a good word for games and does not want to see children overworked.[4] His condemnation of corporal punishment is well known: here again Chrysippus is quoted, this time in disagreement.[5]

Quintilian's system requires that the various subjects of the ἐγκύκλιος παιδεία should be studied concurrently, not one after the other. Mathematics and music are to be learnt whilst the boy is still attending the school of literature;[6] and the first lessons in rhetoric may be taken before he has finally left the *grammaticus* for the *rhetor*.[7] Quintilian is here trying to conciliate public opinion, which was apt to give the *grammaticus* a larger share in the boy's education than Quintilian thought proper. The fault lay mainly with the teachers of rhetoric. Declamation had come to play so large a part in the

[1] *ibid.* i. 1, 15–17.

[2] *ibid.* i. 2, 1. His own son, who died at the age of ten, had studied both Greek and Latin literature (vi, *prooem.* 9–11).

[3] *ibid.* i. 1, 20. [4] *ibid.* 1. 3, 8–13. [5] *ibid.* i. 3, 13–17.

[6] *ibid.* i. 10, 1; 12, 1–7. [7] *ibid.* ii. 1, 13.

course of rhetoric that a fashionable *rhetor* seldom condescended to teach the preparatory exercises in rhetorical composition.[1] This neglect led to two abuses. Either the *grammaticus* took upon himself work which properly belonged to a *rhetor*, thus keeping his boys for an additional year or two; or the first classes in rhetoric were given by some second-rate master whose qualifications did not permit him to teach the more advanced stages of the course.[2] Quintilian condemns both practices. 'It is absurd', he says, 'to keep a boy from the school of declamation until he is able to declaim.' Let each profession respect its neighbour's limits. Some few *grammatici* are, of course, quite competent to teach rhetoric, but this is not their proper work.[3] Suetonius quotes an extreme example. When he was a boy, a certain Princeps used to teach literature and rhetoric on alternate days—sometimes even literature in the morning, rhetoric in the afternoon.[4] Quintilian would have condemned such presumption: less so, however, than the vanity which led many *rhetores* to neglect the elementary part of their course. 'A man is no teacher', he says, 'if he is unwilling to take the lower classes'; and he goes on to argue that the more a man knows about his subject, the better his qualifications for taking a class of beginners.[5]

Here, as elsewhere, Quintilian is speaking from personal experience; for in the following chapter, which describes in detail these preliminary exercises,

[1] Quint. ii. 1, 1–3. [2] *ibid.* ii. 3, 1.
[3] *ibid.* ii. 1, 3–6. [4] Suet. *Gram.* 4. [5] Quint. ii. 3, 5.

he illustrates them by examples taken from his own class-work.[1] And this fact explains an apparent confusion in the *Institutio oratoria* as to the age at which boys attended the schools of rhetoric. Three terms are used by Quintilian to describe his pupils: *pueri*, *adulescentes*, and *iuvenes*. *Iuvenis* is perhaps the commonest of the three, and Quintilian says more than once that he is writing the *Institutio oratoria* for the benefit of *iuvenes*.[2] But *adulescens* is also common;[3] and there is a special warning in the second book against the danger of letting *pueri* sit beside *adulescentes* in class.[4] The same chapter contains a passage in which the custom of applauding a fellow-pupil is more strictly forbidden for *pueri* than for *iuvenes*.[5] Similarly Quintilian tells us that he gave up his reading-classes because older students (*iuvenes*) were beginning to waste time over an exercise which was meant only for the young;[6] and *puer* is the word regularly used in the chapter which deals with the preliminary exercises in rhetoric.[7]

What ages do these various terms denote? Quintilian's chapter on the proper age for beginning the study of rhetoric does not help us much, for he contents himself with the general advice: 'as soon as the boy is able for it'.[8] A more definite statement is contained in the following chapter, where we are told that the boys (*pueri*) who enter a school of

[1] *ibid.* ii. 4, 5–7, 13–14.
[2] *ibid.* i, *prooem.* 1; iii. 6, 64; vi, *prooem.* 1; xii. 11, 31.
[3] *ibid.* v. 12, 22; vii. 3, 30; xii. 11, 13.
[4] *ibid.* ii. 2, 14.
[5] *ibid.* ii. 2, 9.
[6] *ibid.* ii. 5, 1–2.
[7] *ibid.* ii. 4, 1–17; see also x. 5, 1.
[8] *ibid.* ii. 1, 7.

rhetoric are usually in the 'years of adolescence' (*adulti fere*), and that they often stay on as pupils when they are grown men (*iuvenes facti*).[1] Allowing for southern standards, this probably means anything between the ages of fourteen and nineteen: so that Quintilian's experience was mainly of the older type of school-boy. But his words of encouragement for *pueri* who are unused to criticism and easily frightened by harsh correction, show that he had himself learnt from personal experience the value of kindness when dealing with younger boys.[2] Such *pueri* were presumably taught in a separate class, for the exercises which Quintilian prescribes for them are distinct from the more advanced forms of rhetorical composition. The warning that *pueri* should not sit beside *adulescentes* refers most probably to older and younger members of the same class, not to special occasions when the whole school was brought together for a public declamation.[3]

Apart from these practical details of school work Quintilian's account of the ἐγκύκλιος παιδεία is on conventional lines. Music and geometry are to be studied during the course of literature, but Quintilian treats both as subordinate to the study of literature and rhetoric.[4] In the chapter on grammar, for example, we are told that a good *grammaticus* must have studied music: otherwise he will not be able

[1] Quint. ii. 2, 3; see also x. 5, 14; xii. 11, 13.

[2] *ibid.* ii. 4, 8.

[3] *ibid.* ii. 2, 9–10; x. 5, 21 (where the classes are mentioned as separate).

[4] *ibid.* i. 10, 1; 12, 1–19.

to explain the metres of his authors.[1] And in the chapter specially devoted to music at the end of the first book, after some generalities borrowed from Greek educational theorists—with quotations from Pythagoras, Lycurgus, Plato, Archytas, and Aristoxenus [2]—Quintilian comes to the practical question: how will music benefit the orator? The answer is severely practical: it will teach him to control and modulate his voice, and make harmonious gestures.[3] Similarly, geometry is to be studied partly for the excellent mental training that it gives, partly for its practical utility when the orator has to speak of such subjects as land-measurement or more intricate mathematical problems: it would never do for him to hesitate in public over his figures.[4] But neither music nor geometry is to be studied with a specialist's care; [5] and the same principle is applied to the lessons in elocution which Quintilian expects the boy to get from some professional actor.[6]

Quintilian's main interest is, of course, in the schools of literature and rhetoric, Greek and Latin. The boy should go first to the Greek *grammaticus*; [7] but both literatures are taught concurrently, and in the same way. There are lessons in the spoken language (*recte loquendi scientia*), which include dictation and composition as well as grammar, and lessons in the literature of both languages (*poetarum*

[1] *ibid.* i. 4, 4; 10, 28–9. [2] *ibid.* i. 10, 9–21.
[3] *ibid.* i. 10, 22–30; see also xi. 3, 14–65.
[4] *ibid.* i. 10, 34–49. [5] *ibid.* i. 12, 14.
[6] *ibid.* i. 11, 1–14; xi. 3, 88–91, 181. [7] *ibid.* i. 4, 1.

enarratio).[1] A more detailed definition of the work done by the *grammaticus* is given casually in an earlier chapter: he teaches his pupil how to speak correctly, explains grammatical difficulties in the authors read, interprets historical allusions and comments on his author.[2] Quintilian's enthusiasm for the study of grammar is well known,[3] and was probably due to the influence of Remmius Palaemon. His chapter on the authors to be read at school is shorter, probably in view of the later digression on the same subject which fills half of the tenth book. Homer and Virgil are in a class by themselves; but the tragedians, comedians, and lyric poets are all mentioned as suitable school-texts.[4] Quintilian is, of course, severely classical in his tastes, but does not exclude the older Latin poets from his list, probably out of respect for Cicero's known preferences.[5] Elsewhere, however, he is hard on the early Latin prose-writers.[6] And his moral standards are no less exacting. Menander can be read safely by boys, but the other comedians are mentioned with reserve: even Horace should not be read in class unexpurgated.[7]

The study of prose-authors raises once more the interesting question: how much history was read at school? Quintilian expects the *grammaticus* to explain such historical and mythological allusions as occur in his text;[8] but experience had taught him

[1] Quint. i. 4, 2. [2] *ibid.* i. 2, 14. [3] *ibid.* i. 4, 5–6.
[4] *ibid.* i. 8, 5–7. [5] *ibid.* i. 8, 8–12. [6] *ibid.* ii. 5, 21–3.
[7] *ibid.* i. 8, 6, 7. [8] *ibid.* i. 2, 14; 4, 4; 8. 18–21.

that this kind of teaching was apt to end in a pedantic display of erudition. ‘ It is sufficient ’, he says, ‘ to explain well-known legends, or such at least as are told by the standard authors ’ ; and he ends with the sensible remark that ‘ a good teacher will not know everything ’.[1] Plainly the fact that prose-authors were not read as school-texts left something to be desired, and Quintilian was conscious of this *lacuna* in the ‘ encyclic ’ programme. In his second book he tells us of an experiment which he had made by way of supplementing this part of the course in Greek and Latin literature. Greek teachers of rhetoric usually arranged for reading-classes to be given by an assistant-master (*adiutor* or *hypodidascalus*), the great masters of Greek prose being the texts read.[2] Quintilian approves of this system, but suggests an improvement. Such lessons should not be mere reading-classes, but should be used as an extension of the earlier classes in poetic literature. The boys should be made read aloud in turn and the *rhetor* himself—not an assistant-master—should be there to interrupt, correct, point out the good or bad points in the author's style, and ask the pupils for their own opinion.[3] Organized on these lines the class could easily be got to read and criticize specimens of the best orators and historians in Greek and Latin : Cicero and Livy are named as the authors most suitable for the purpose.[4] Quintilian himself had tried the experiment in his school, but had found that custom was against him, and that

[1] *ibid.* i. 8, 18, 21.
[2] *ibid.* ii. 5, 3 ; Cic. *ad Fam.* ix. 18, 4.
[3] *ibid.* ii. 5, 1–17.
[4] *ibid.* ii. 5, 18–19.

the wrong kind of pupil was showing interest in the work. For these reasons he had abandoned the system, but leaves the experiment on record for the benefit of future teachers.[1]

§ 3. *Rhetoric : the 'Declamationes'.*

The transition from literature to rhetoric was marked by a series of preparatory exercises in composition, which Quintilian describes in some detail. The Greek term for all these exercises was *progymnasmata*, and text-books for this portion of the ἐγκύκλιος παιδεία still survive: notably the *Progymnasmata* of Theon. Quintilian assigns some of these exercises to the *grammaticus*, others to the *rhetor*.[2] Even quite young boys could easily do the earliest and simplest. One of Aesop's fables was read aloud, and the boy was then asked to tell the story himself in simple, correct language.[3] Later he was made write the story down in the same simple style; and another favourite exercise was the free paraphrase in prose of a passage taken from some poet read in class.[4] Greek teachers passed directly from these simpler forms of composition to the *narratio*, taking their subject-matter either from poetry or history.[5] Quintilian reserves the *narratio* for a later stage, and passes from the fable and paraphrase to the *sententia* and *chria*. These were short compositions on some proverb or saying of a great man, the *sententia* being impersonal, the *chria* connected with some historical

[1] Quint. ii. 5, 2.
[2] *ibid.* i. 9, 1–6; ii. 4, 1–40.
[3] *ibid.* i. 9 2.
[4] *ibid.*
[5] Colson on Quint. i. 9, 6.

personality.[1] *Sunt lacrimae rerum* is an obvious example. A *chria* on this verse would begin by paraphrasing the meaning, then give the reasons for and against, illustrate the verse from its context in the *Aeneid* and from other historical examples, confirm it by quotations from the poets, and end with a formal *epilogue*.

Quintilian assigns all these *progymnasmata* to the *grammaticus*: those which he enumerates in the second book belong properly to the *rhetor*, though in practice they were often taught by the *grammaticus*. For Quintilian complains that, in the Latin schools at least, teachers of rhetoric had allowed the *grammatici* to usurp this part of their course.[2] The question is of some importance as these later exercises include practice in historical composition. Quintilian, who read the historians in class with his pupils, places historical *narratio* first on the list of *progymnasmata* reserved for the teacher of rhetoric.[3] His purpose, it should be noted, is not primarily to impart knowledge of history; and his suggestions deal mainly with questions of style. But historical compositions can easily be made to follow a definite plan of reading, and Quintilian does not need to be told that exercises in style are doubly useful when connected with the authors read in class.[4] Indeed some of the subjects which he suggests for exercises akin to *narratio* are taken straight from Livy.[5]

[1] *ibid.* i. 9, 3 with Colson's valuable notes.

[2] *ibid.* i. 9, 6; ii. 1, 1–2.

[3] *ibid.* ii. 4, 1–3, 15–19.

[4] *ibid.* i. 9, 3; ii. 5, 14–17.

[5] *ibid.* ii. 4, 18, 19.

A natural sequel to these *narrationes* were compositions in praise of great men or in condemnation of the wicked, and formal comparisons between two or more famous personages: an exercise which gave Plutarch the idea for his *Parallel Lives*.[1] These exercises border on what was technically considered rhetoric, and Quintilian follows them up with *loci communes* and *theses*; the former being essays on this or that type of character, the latter more abstract themes such as 'Country-life and Town-life', or a comparison between the work of a lawyer and a soldier.[2] Lastly he names a type of composition even more directly useful to the orator: set passages (*loci*) on the value of evidence, the justice or injustice of laws, their opportuneness and so forth.[3] The student who has mastered this type of composition is ready for either *suasoriae* or *controversiae*.[4]

This well-ordered sequence of *progymnasmata* gives a fair idea of ancient rhetoric at its best. Whatever its faults, Greek rhetoric as it had been elaborated by Aristotle, Hermagoras and their successors was a carefully planned, logical system of education; and its minutest details had been thought out by teachers who formed their theories for themselves in the class-room. No attempt can be made here to describe the system as a whole: there is no short cut through it and Quintilian is still the best author on the subject. Indeed, the main portion of the *Institutio oratoria* was planned by Quintilian as a

[1] Quint. ii. 4, 20–1.
[2] *ibid.* ii. 4, 22–5; x. 5, 11–13.
[3] *ibid.* ii. 4, 27–40.
[4] *ibid.* ii. 4, 33.

sort of encyclopedia of ancient rhetoric. In his prefatory letter to Trypho he explains that the book had taken him two years to write: not because he found writing difficult, but because he had to 'examine an almost endless subject and read innumerable authorities'.[1] A long list of these 'authorities' is to be found at the beginning of the third book: it begins with Empedocles, and ends with the elder Pliny and his contemporaries.[2] Modern research has taught us to be cautious in accepting such literary catalogues as proof that the compiler of the catalogue has read all the authors named; and Quintilian's list is plainly inserted *eruditionis causa.* Some of the earlier names are admittedly given at second-hand, and there are good reasons for believing that Quintilian owed his knowledge even of Aristotle's *Rhetoric* to quotations which he had found in later Greek writers: Aristotle was for centuries little more than a name to educated Greeks and Romans.[3] But Aristotle had many successors: Theophrastus, Hermagoras, Apollonius, Caecilius, Dionysius, Apollodorus, and Theodorus, to name only the most famous—and Quintilian is here on ground that he knows well. His theory of rhetoric is indeed no more than an intelligent compilation from the writings of these Greek theorists, and he himself apologizes for his lack of originality.[4] His aim was rather to give his readers a sound professional judgement where, as usually happened, the

[1] *ibid. praef. ad Tryph.* 1.

[2] *ibid.* iii. 1, 8–21.

[3] Angermann, pp. 28 foll.

[4] Quint. iii. 1, 5.

'authorities' disagreed among themselves: common sense, painstaking accuracy in the statement of received opinions and remarkable clearness in the exposition of his own views are perhaps the chief merits of his work:

'I shall not be afraid', he says himself, 'to give my own opinion when needed, though so many have written well on this subject. Nor have I slavishly followed the teaching of any one school, but have left my readers free to choose what view they think best, my task being rather to gather into a single volume the results of many workers. Where there was no room left for further discovery, I have been content with the reputation of work thoroughly done.' [1]

Quintilian prefaces his treatise on rhetoric with an introductory chapter on the value of declamation. So many loose statements have been made about this portion of his educational theory that his views are better quoted in full.

'Declamation', he says, 'is the most modern of all our exercises, and also by far the most useful. For it contains in itself all those preparatory exercises which I have described, and comes as near to real life as a representation can. That is why it has become so popular, and is now commonly thought sufficient of itself to make an orator; for no quality of sustained oratory is absent from this systematic exercise in speaking. Unfortunately—thanks to bad teaching—matters have been let go so far that the ignorance and extravagance of our declaimers is now a main cause of our decadent oratory; but it is permissible to make good use of what is by nature good. The subjects set for development should, I hold, be modelled closely on real life, and declamation, which was invented as an exercise for public speaking, should imitate public speaking as far as possible.' [2]

Like most of what Quintilian has written, this is plain common sense; and he goes on to develop

[1] Quint. iii. 1, 22. [2] *ibid.* ii. 10, 1–4.

certain obvious lessons. School-declamations dealt mainly with fictitious and romantic situations: witches, oracles, plagues, cruel stepmothers, and so forth were part of the ordinary stock-in-trade. Quintilian does not bar these fictions absolutely, but he wants them kept within reasonable limits. A certain amount of romance is no bad thing for boys who will let themselves go more easily when the subject is romantic; but the fiction should never become ridiculous, and there should always be close contact with real life.[1] Quintilian never wearies of insisting on this point: declamation that has ceased to be a training for the forum is like a theatrical display or the ravings of a lunatic. 'What is the use', he asks, 'of conciliating the judge when there is no judge; of narrating what is plainly false; of proving a case which will never come up for decision?'[2] And he has more than negative criticism to offer—though his suggestions are put forward tentatively with the feeling that custom is against him. He would like, for example, to see the declamations made more concrete: proper names should be used, as had once been the rule.[3] Then the plots should be made more complicated, less crudely obvious; and the language should be less artificial, more akin to the speech of everyday life.[4] *Sententiae* are all very well and there is no lack of them in the *Institutio oratoria*; but Quintilian knows the danger of abuse, and more than once speaks out

[1] *ibid.* ii. 10, 5–6; v. 12, 17–23.
[2] *ibid.* ii. 10, 8.
[3] *ibid.* ii. 10, 9; Suet. *rhet.* 1.
[4] *ibid.* ii. 10, 9; viii. 3, 23.

openly on the subject.[1] Nor was this the only fault in these artificial declamations. A joke would seem out of place in most of the *controversiae* described by the elder Seneca, and jokes are none too plentiful in the *Institutio oratoria* which is truly Spanish in its *gravitas*. But Quintilian is careful to remind us that no lawyer can do without an occasional jest, and he has a special chapter *de Risu*.[2] Some of these faults were of course inherent in the system of school-declamation, but Quintilian insists that good teaching will cure most of them; and he ends his chapter with an ingenious comparison. On the stage actors avoid the tone of ordinary conversation, but their art consists in remaining natural whilst adopting a convention. Similarly declamation, which is primarily intended to be a reproduction of public oratory, should imitate real life without losing that 'epideictic' quality which marks it off from ordinary speech.[3]

Quintilian's attitude towards declamation can be illustrated from every portion of his work. In the first chapter of the second book, for example, the teacher of rhetoric is called *magister declamandi* from his most important class.[4] The next chapter deals with the duties of a teacher, and stress is laid on the need for authority, tact, patience, and kindness in the difficult work of controlling a class of excitable and sensitive boys, who are apt to have their heads turned by a successful declamation.[5] The need for

[1] Quint. ii. 4, 31; viii. 5, 34. [2] *ibid.* ii. 10, 9; vi. 3, 1.
[3] *ibid.* ii. 10, 10–13. [4] *ibid.* ii. 1, 3. [5] *ibid.* ii. 2, 4–13.

tact and firmness in correcting faults is reiterated in a later chapter of the same book: some of the pupils will not like it, but the class as a whole will suffer if the fault goes uncorrected.[1] And yet another chapter discusses a delicate question: how far should a teacher let each pupil develop according to his natural bent? Quintilian recognizes the value of natural aptitudes, but cannot see why the child's latent possibilities should not be developed as well as his more obvious gifts. If a boy has no gift for oratory, let him be sent home; but those who mean to prepare for the forum will have to work hard, for oratory requires every gift that a man has or can acquire.[2]

All this is sound psychology, and Quintilian's practical experience is plain in later allusions to the same question. How long should a boy be kept at the exercise of declamation? Quintilian protests against the custom of certain teachers who keep their boys for ever at school: partly from the false idea that declamation is an end in itself, partly from greed of larger profits.[3] His own advice is that work in the forum should be begun as soon as the young man has sufficient confidence in his powers to risk the venture: he can then come back to his master for advice and correction.[4] This will keep the school in contact with real life, and Quintilian cites the example of Porcius Latro as a warning to those

[1] *ibid.* ii. 6, 3–5.
[2] *ibid.* ii. 8; x. 2, 19–21.
[3] *ibid.* ii. 20, 4; xii. 11, 14.
[4] *ibid.* xii. 6, 1–7; xii. 11, 15–16.

who think that school-declamations are enough of themselves to make an orator.[1]

Can we go further, and illustrate Quintilian's precepts from his own example? Once at least in the *Institutio oratoria* Quintilian interrupts the technical exposition of his theory to develop in detail the plot of a school-declamation.[2] The plot itself is of some interest as showing the type of *controversia* which Quintilian was accustomed to declaim. 'Some young men, who had the habit of dining together, arranged for a supper on the sea-shore. One of them misses the supper, and the others inscribe his name on a tomb which they have built for him. His father, who has been travelling overseas, lands on that part of the shore, reads his son's name and hangs himself. The young men are accused of having caused his death.' Fantastic though it may sound, that is a typical *controversia*; and Quintilian discusses it quite seriously. There is first an analysis (*finitio*) of the case for prosecution, then of the case for defence: then a brief development of the main arguments to be urged on either side with due regard for the probabilities of the case. Nobody has ever questioned the authenticity of this passage from the *Institutio oratoria*: yet it has an important bearing on a question which has much vexed modern students of Quintilian's theory. Did Quintilian write all or any of the *Declamationes* which have come down to us under his name? A brief statement of the main facts at issue will help to explain the problem, and

[1] Quint. x. 5, 17–21; see above, p. 167. [2] *ibid.* vii. 3, 30–4.

may throw further light on the work done in the schools of Latin rhetoric.

Two sets of declamations ascribed to Quintilian have survived, each with its separate manuscript tradition. One is complete and is known as the *Declamationes maiores* : it consists of nineteen school declamations, worked out in full as models of the *genre.* Some of the titles are suggestive of the contents: 'The Wall with the Fingermarks' (*Paries palmatus*), 'The Blind Man at the Door,' 'A Soldier of Marius,' 'The Astrologer,' and so forth. As it stands, the collection must have been put together before the end of the fourth century A.D.; for the manuscript tradition can be traced back to an archetype of that period, and there are numerous quotations from these declamations in writers of the fourth and fifth centuries.[1] Most of these authors quote the *Declamationes* as the work of Quintilian, and there are also quotations from two other declamations by Quintilian, not included in our collection: the *Fanaticus* and the *Caput involutum.*[2] Nevertheless, Quintilian is almost certainly not the author of the *Declamationes maiores.* The style is unlike his careful moderation; the themes chosen are just those against which he warns young students; and they are made even more extravagant by the author's taste for the fantastic. Those who have studied the *Declamationes maiores* in detail are agreed that they belong most probably to the second

[1] Ritter, pp. 204 foll.; Schanz, ii. 2, p. 464, 467.
[2] Lact. *Div. inst.* i. 21; v. 7.

century A.D. Apuleius seems to have known them;[1] and Trebellius Pollio, writing towards the end of the third century, refers to declamations by Quintilian which ranked as the best of their kind.[2]

So far there is little difficulty. The *Declamationes maiores* were probably produced in the Latin schools of rhetoric some time after Quintilian's death, and were attributed to the famous *rhetor* as a guarantee of their excellence: that seems a fair hypothesis, and most scholars accept it as the most probable explanation of the facts. But a different theory is needed to explain the origin of a second collection of declamations attributed to Quintilian, the *Declamationes minores*. To begin with, more than half of this collection—and that the first half—is missing in all our manuscripts. There is no title-page, though numerous *subscriptiones* testify to Quintilian's authorship; and the preface, if there was one, is also missing. The loss is serious, for the *Declamationes minores* certainly need some kind of a preface. Unlike the *Declamationes maiores* they are not worked out in full; nor are they mere extracts from complete declamations, like the elder Seneca's *Sententiae et Colores*. For the most part they give no more than an outline of the plan to be developed, with an occasional more elaborate specimen. Sometimes this outline or specimen is given without further comment; more frequently the *declamatio* is interrupted by an oral commentary—headed *Sermo*

[1] Weyman in *Sitzber. d. bay. Ak.*, ph.-hist. Kl. ii. (1893), p. 287.
[2] Trebell. Pollio, *Vit. Post. jun.* 4, 2.

in our manuscripts—which contains practical suggestions for the development of the argument, or remarks about the psychology of the situation; sometimes the *sermo* comes at the beginning, and serves as a sort of introduction to the *declamatio* proper; and there are some *sermones* without any *declamatio*. In all, there are still extant 145 declamations, and more than half of these have the *sermo* in one form or another.

What are we to make of so curious a text? One fact is certain: this mixture of *sermo* and *declamatio* was only possible in a class-room, and the *Declamationes minores* are most easily explained as the notes either of a master or a student. But are they the work of Quintilian or notes taken in class by one of his pupils? The manuscript tradition is here the only external evidence available, for no ancient author quotes from the *Declamationes minores*; and the manuscript tradition brings us no further back than the ninth or tenth century.[1] On the other hand, the very form of the book suggests an indirect argument as to its authorship. Class-notes are not the sort of work most likely to attract attention. If these class-notes were first published without Quintilian's name, no later scribe was likely to claim them as the work of so famous an author; and if Quintilian's name was deliberately forged by the author, there remains a further difficulty. Why was he not careful to make his book more obviously the sort of book which Quintilian might have written?

[1] Ritter, p. 252; Schanz, ii. 2, p. 464.

For the *Declamationes minores* give the critic a twofold problem to solve. On the one hand, the matter of both *sermones* and *declamationes* is excellent, and the care spent on the arrangement and analysis of the plot (*divisio* and *finitio*) is in strict accordance with Quintilian's principles.[1] The language, too, is correct; and the style—when not disjointed by the peculiar form of the text—is very much in Quintilian's manner. But no reader can resist the impression that Quintilian would never have passed these notes for publication. There is no attempt at bringing the material into any sort of systematic order, and the unevenness of the style is sometimes inexcusable.[2] The simplest solution of the difficulty is to suppose that these are the class-notes of one of Quintilian's pupils, published either without his consent during his lifetime or after his death. Quintilian himself complains that two sets of class-notes had already been published before the appearance of the *Institutio oratoria.*[3] The earlier had been taken down hurriedly during two days by some of his younger pupils: a description which could not possibly suit the *Declamationes minores*, originally 388 in number. But Quintilian's description of the second set, whether it refers to our extant collection or not, exactly describes its character. 'The second', he says, 'was taken down as fully as possible in shorthand during several days, and was then

[1] Quint. ii. 6; vii. 3; 4; Ritter, pp. 225 foll.

[2] Leo, p. 117 (quoting *Decl.* 247, 268, 270, 306 as specimens).

[3] Quint. i, *prooem.* 7.

published in a hurry by young students who meant well, but were over-eager in their loyalty to me.'

Granted that the *Declamationes minores* may well be a product of Quintilian's class-room, it is interesting to see what light they throw on his methods of teaching. One or two coincidences are worth noting. Quintilian twice refers to a *declamatio* on the following topic: 'A man has three sons: an orator, a philosopher, and a doctor. He divides his property into four parts, leaving one to each and the fourth to the one who has proved himself most useful to the state. The sons dispute for the property.'[1] This *declamatio* is included in the *Declamationes minores*, and the doctor is made to state his case against the two others: it is an interesting specimen of a very conventional theme.[2] Two other plots are common to the *Declamationes* in their present incomplete form and the *Institutio oratoria*. One is entitled *Adulter sacerdos* and is as follows: 'Priests have the right of freeing one man from sentence of death; adultery is to be punished by death. A priest is taken in adultery and claims immunity for himself by reason of his privilege. He is killed, and his slayer is accused of murder.'[3] The other is even more fantastic: 'The law requires that he who violates a woman should die within thirty days, unless he obtain pardon from his own and the woman's father. A man has sinned, and obtains pardon from the woman's

[1] *ibid.* vii. 1, 38; 4, 39.
[2] *Decl.* 268.
[3] Quint. v. 10, 104 (= *decl.* 284).

father, but is refused by his own parent. He accuses his father of madness.' [1]

These coincidences between the *Institutio* and the *Declamationes* are mainly interesting for the light they throw on Quintilian's attitude towards the conventional school-declamations : he does not reject them, but seeks to use them in a rational way. And certainly no reader of the *Declamationes minores* can fail to detect a note of sincerity in all that is said by this anonymous schoolmaster. Many of the *sermones* are admirable in their own way,[2] and the *declamationes*, however extravagant the subjects proposed, are notable examples of restraint, well-ordered arrangement of the argument, and sound psychology. Quotation from the *declamationes* is impossible, but here is a typical *sermo* : the subject proposed is one which must have made a special appeal to Quintilian.[3]

'The law allows a man to demand an advocate. Ingratitude is a criminal offence. A rich man has sent a poor young man to Athens at his own expense : he returns an orator. A *delator* accuses the rich man of treason, and demands as his advocate the poor student whom the rich man had educated. The poor man pleads in court, and loses the case. The rich man sues him for ingratitude.'

Sermo.

'You understand that this young man must show the greatest respect for his rich patron : that is the way to make it plain that he is acting under necessity, should any complaint be made about his conduct. And this rule should be generally observed in all *controversiae* which deal with charges of ingratitude : we must be careful not to make the accused appear ungrateful in his speech. Only very seldom will you meet with a *controversia* in

1 Quint. ix. 2, 90 (= *Decl.* 349).

2 See esp. *Decl.* 270, 316, 338, 349, 351–9.

3 *ibid.* 333.

which it is open to question whether the man accused of ingratitude ever received a benefit. Most of them, as here, can be reduced to the following questions. Is every man ungrateful who has received a benefit, and has failed to requite it? Was the man bound to answer every call on his gratitude? Was he able to do so?

'Those who are greedy of novel situations will easily be tempted here to make the poor man suggest that the rich man is acting in collusion with himself. But were the jury to believe this, they would either sentence him for his own share in the collusion or else for his ingratitude on this occasion, when he is not bound to appear in the courts and yet accuses his patron by insinuating that his own acquittal will be due to collusion. Therefore, as far as my judgement goes, the case is one in which the poor man is unwilling to appear; what he says, he says under stress of circumstances.'

The *declamatio* which follows develops the points suggested in the *sermo*: Lysias himself could not have been more true to the *ethos* of the situation. And it is interesting to compare the plea of duress put forward to justify the poor man's action in the earlier law-suit with Quintilian's advice to a young advocate on the question of defending a client who is plainly in the wrong.[1] The style too, with its short sentences and power of concise statement, is very like Quintilian's; and the Latin is correct—with one or two exceptions where the text is doubtful.[2] Some of the other *sermones* suggest Quintilian's thought and manner no less plainly. In one the theory of *finitio* is stated in words almost identical with a corresponding passage in the *Institutio oratoria*;[3]

[1] Quint. xii. 7, 6–7.

[2] As a rule it is safer not to accept the emendations printed in Ritter's text.

[3] *Decl.* 247 (= Quint. vii. 3, 19–23).

another gives a comparison between the *exordium* and *epilogue* of a *declamatio* which is well worth comparing with Quintilian's chapter on the need for an *exordium* in public oratory;[1] and elsewhere the *scholastica materia* of a school declamation is contrasted with the *forense opus* of a public orator,[2] a contrast which underlies all Quintilian's theory of rhetoric.

Whoever their author, these *Declamationes minores* are valuable as evidence of the way in which ancient rhetoric was taught. In all the *Institutio oratoria* there is only one direct reference to the declamations which Quintilian must have given every day at school. As an instance of what a good memory can do, Quintilian mentions the fact that when some distinguished visitors entered his class-room—a common occurrence in the Latin schools of rhetoric[3]—he was always able to repeat word for word the extemporary declamation which had been interrupted by their arrival.[4] The *Declamationes* take us straight into such a class-room and show us how rhetoric was taught by men like Quintilian. 'I must show you the way', the anonymous teacher says in one of the *sermones*: 'first find out what each party is aiming at, what their arguments are: then state those arguments as briefly and as clearly as possible'; and he follows up his precept with a practical illustration of how it should be done.[5] This is in strict accordance with Quintilian's advice:

[1] *Decl.* 338 (= Quint. iv. 1; esp. 3–4). [2] *ibid.* 325, 338.
[3] Pliny, *Epp.* ii. 18; vi. 6, 3; Bornecque, p. 55.
[4] Quint. xi. 2, 39. [5] *Decl.* 247.

'The teacher should every day say something—or rather many things—which his pupils may retain in their memories. For, though reading will supply them with any number of models to imitate, nevertheless the teacher's own words—his "living voice" as the phrase goes—gives them more substantial nourishment: above all, if the teacher be a man whom well-educated pupils will love and venerate. It is amazing how much more willing we are to imitate those for whom we have a liking.' [1]

Indeed, it would be hard not to have a liking both for Quintilian and for the author of the *Declamationes*. Here is the latter's apology for what might seem unnecessary repetition:

'If I sometimes repeat the same thing several times over in my analysis of these *controversiae*, remember that I do so partly for the sake of the new-comers, partly because the analysis involves repetition. For those who were not at the earlier classes must be taught the general principles which are applicable to all *controversiae*, and analysis (*divisio*) is especially important in the kind of *controversia* which we are now doing.' [2]

A little later there is another apology, equally reminiscent of Quintilian's manner:

'I do not want any one to complain that I am not giving you an opportunity for purple patches (*loci*). You can develop this declamation if you like and show off your talent; but you will be making a speech that may perhaps be pleasing to the ear, but will certainly have nothing to do with the subject set.' [3]

The subject set was the following. 'A father insists on following his prodigal son through the public streets in tears: he is charged with madness.' Were ancient teachers of rhetoric altogether wrong in setting such subjects for their students? May it not well be a fine achievement of education to teach a boy

[1] Quint. ii. 2, 8. [2] *Decl.* 314.
[3] *ibid.* 316 (p. 244, Ritter); compare Quint. x. 5, 22.

that even the most dramatic situation loses none of its effectiveness by being stated clearly in simple, dignified language ?

§ 4. *Supplementary Studies.*

Quintilian's theory of rhetoric occupies seven books (III–IX) of his *Institutio oratoria.* There is no use in pretending that these seven books make light reading, though the great *rhetor's* pupils seem to have prized them more highly than any other part of their master's work. To the modern reader they are as uninviting as an ordinary text-book of Formal Logic : 'a bare statement of rules', as Quintilian himself warns his readers with a tactful quotation from Lucretius.[1] Here and there, of course, passages can be found which have more than a technical interest : the chapter on joking as a fine art is worth comparing with Cicero's digression on the same subject,[2] and those who enjoy the unravelling of complicated word-puzzles should see what they can make of Quintilian's section on prose-rhythm.[3] But it is only in the tenth book that Quintilian regains the easy conversational manner which is his when he is at his best. None but a pedant could feel that the arid questions of detail and rhetorical technique which make so much of the *Institutio oratoria* difficult reading, contain the real stuff of oratory. Quintilian knows better than that: his ninth book ends with a hurried paragraph, and the opening words of his next chapter

[1] Quint. iii. 1, 2–4.
[2] *ibid.* vi. 3 ; Cic. *de Or.* ii. 235–89. [3] Quint. ix. 4, 45–111.

carry the 'Education of an Orator' forward to its last and most important stage. How can a student who has already mastered the formal precepts of rhetoric acquire the easy sureness of habit ?[1]

Quintilian is following, more or less consciously, the general principles of Cicero's *de Oratore.* The question with which this tenth book of the *Institutio oratoria* opens should thus mark the transition from Cicero's *puerilis institutio*, with its studies in literature and rhetoric, to the more mature culture of his *politior humanitas.* But a striking coincidence of phrase which occurs in this same chapter shows how far Quintilian is from the true spirit of Ciceronian *humanitas.* Cicero had based his programme of higher studies on the general principle that an orator must possess abundance of matter (*copia rerum*), if he is to acquire and master an abundant vocabulary (*copia verborum*).[2] Quintilian enuntiates what is at first sight the same principle. 'The orator', he says, 'must be possessed of certain resources which he can use when necessary: these are abundance of matter and words (*copia rerum ac verborum*).'[3] But his development of this doctrine differs surprisingly from Cicero's theory. The matter of oratory, he argues, will depend on the particular subject of discussion. What is wanted is a ready command of vocabulary; and that can only be acquired by wide reading in Greek and Latin literature.[4] In other words, Quintilian's programme of

[1] *ibid.* x. 1, 1.
[2] Cic. *de Or.* iii. 125; above, p. 113.
[3] Quint. x. 1, 5.
[4] *ibid.* x. 1, 6–8.

higher studies is no more than a continuation of the literary course already given by the *grammaticus* and *rhetor*.

Generations of classical scholars have turned with pleasure to the tenth book of the *Institutio oratoria*; and there is no denying that Quintilian is at his best, or almost at his best, as a literary critic. The famous series of parallels between Greek and Latin literature may not be always original in the criticisms which they contain; but those criticisms are always discerning and always agreeably phrased. Yet to one who reads the *Institutio oratoria* as a whole this tenth book comes as a disappointment. Compared with those portions of the *de Oratore* in which Cicero describes his *politior humanitas*, the literary counsels of the great schoolmaster are too obviously reminiscent of the class-room. Year after year Quintilian's pupil has sat on the benches, listening to the lectures of *grammaticus*, *rhetor*, and every other professor of the ἐγκύκλιος παιδεία. Now that his freedom is in sight, he is bidden take up his books again: tablet in hand—for Quintilian does not neglect even that detail[1]—he is to re-read his classics, note their individual excellences, criticize and compare one with another, above all busy himself with the imitation of their style. *Studendum vero semper et ubique.*[2] That is Quintilian's final word of advice, and he promises to the student who has been faithful to that golden rule an achievement which he describes as 'the most precious fruit of all our studies and the noble reward

[1] Quint. x. 1, 20; 3, 31–3. [2] *ibid.* x. 7, 27.

of our years of labour': the power of delivering a well-balanced, well-phrased, fluent speech on any ordinary subject with a minimum of preparation.[1]

All of this could, of course, be paralleled, from the *de Oratore*, or indeed from any ancient author who discusses the question of literary composition. But the emphasis is different in Cicero's dialogue: his *politior humanitas* connotes something more than refinement of literary taste. And the contrast is made more striking by what has all the appearance of an afterthought in Quintilian's twelfth book. Towards the end of his preface to the first book Quintilian outlines the plan of his work.

> 'The first book', he tells us, 'will contain those studies which precede the work of the *rhetor*; in the second we shall treat of the first elementary instruction given in the school of rhetoric and of the questions which concern the substance of rhetoric. The next five books will be given to *inventio*, to which I have added the proper ordering of one's matter (*dispositio*). Four more will be devoted to style, memory and delivery. Finally one will be added in which we shall perfect the orator himself, discussing to the best of our powers his moral character; the method to be observed in undertaking, studying and defending a legal case; the right type of eloquence; the most suitable time for ending a public career; the studies best suited for the end of life.'[2]

With one exception, this is an exact description of the matter contained in the *Institutio oratoria*: the greater detail given concerning the matter of the

[1] *ibid.* x. 7, 1–4, 12.

[2] *ibid.* i, *prooem.* 21–2. My attention was first drawn to this passage by Beltrami's article in *Studi italiani di filologia classica*, xix (1912), pp. 63–72.

twelfth book is explained by the novelty which Quintilian himself claims for this portion of his programme.[1] But the exception is worth noting. After the first chapter of the twelfth book, in which Quintilian discusses the moral character of his perfect orator, three chapters are inserted on the advantages to be derived from a study of philosophy, jurisprudence, and history.[2] These are, he tells us, the orator's instruments, the weapons which he must have ever ready to hand for use in the fray ; always presupposing that ready command of vocabulary and metaphor, that knowledge of *inventio* and *dispositio*, that power of memory and graceful delivery which have been scientifically provided for in the first eleven books of the *Institutio oratoria*.[3] The rest of the twelfth book then follows in detail the plan already outlined, and ends with a brief account of the occupations suitable for an orator who has retired from public life.[4]

Now why should Quintilian have made this curious insertion at the very end of his work ? Why begin all over again a programme of higher studies which has apparently already been completed ? An answer to these questions may be found in the short *Prooemium* to the twelfth book. Here Quintilian affects a momentary alarm at the horizon which is opening before him. *Caelum undique et undique*

[1] Quint. xii, *prooem*. 3–4.

[2] *ibid*. xii. 2 ; 3 ; 4.

[3] *ibid*. xii. 5, 1.

[4] *ibid*. xii. 11, 1–7. The rest of the chapter is a formal ' Epilogue ' to the whole work.

pontus. Hitherto he has had the guidance of those who had written either manuals of rhetoric or essays on literary style. Now there is only Cicero—and even Cicero is at best a partial guide. For the purpose of this twelfth book is to follow the orator on his course through public life, 'now that he has gone from the schools of rhetoric and is either borne along by his own vigour or seeks a nobler ally in the very temple of wisdom'.[1] In other words, Quintilian, who frequently speaks in metaphors when he has some weakness to conceal, is more than usually dependent on Cicero's *de Oratore* for the matter of his twelfth book; and he probably became uneasily conscious that his original plan excluded some of the most characteristic features of Cicero's educational theory. So he adds at the last moment a hurried chapter or two in which he discusses those portions of Cicero's theory with which he was himself least in sympathy. There is even a clumsy attempt to fit this later addition into the original plan of his book without appearing to do so. At the end of Book II Quintilian had reserved for this portion of the twelfth book a discussion of certain *instrumenta artis rhetoricae* which, he maintains, are more properly defined as *instrumenta oratoris.*[2] Presence of mind, a powerful voice, physical health and beauty: these are the principal *instrumenta* which he names in the corresponding passage of his twelfth book. They should, of course, have been given separate treatment;

[1] *ibid.* xii, *prooem.* 3.
[2] *ibid.* ii. 21, 24.
[3] *ibid.* xii. 5, 1–6.

but they are in fact classed with the study of philosophy, history, and law as *instrumenta non artis, sed oratoris.*[1] Even a skilled artist cannot always conceal his inconsistencies!

No reader of these parenthetical chapters can fail to note the difference between Cicero's enthusiastic plea for his three favourite studies and Quintilian's brief discussion of their merits. The chapter on philosophy had best be reserved for comparison with Quintilian's theory of the ideal orator: it is full of half-grudging admissions, and gives one the impression of an ungrateful task got through as best may be. The chapter which urges the necessity of legal knowledge for a practising lawyer develops a commonplace theme with Quintilian's usual common sense, but there is no touch of personal enthusiasm: those who turn away from oratory to law are treated as cowards who have despaired of success in the nobler profession.[2] And the study of history is dismissed in three brief sentences, with the traditional comment that oratory is always more effective when illustrated by examples from the past.[3] This from an author who had already found space for an excursus on the study of grammar which covers more than twenty pages of his first book! And it is no mere accident of personal taste that Cicero should have been an enthusiast for history, Quintilian for grammar. It is the old contrast between the student

[1] Quint. xii. 5, 1.

[2] *ibid.* xii. 3, 9. The whole chapter should be compared with Cic., *de Or.* i. 166–203, 234–55.

[3] Quint. xii. 4.

who is also a man of the world and the student who knows and loves only his books. 'A love for letters (*grammatice*) and the habit of reading do not end with our school-days, but are lifelong possessions': the phrase, which occurs in the first book of the *Institutio oratoria*,[1] sums up Quintilian's intellectual aspirations.

It is in the tenth book, then, that Quintilian's *politior humanitas* is best expressed, and for that very reason the book has never lacked readers among those who love the classics. For Quintilian is the typical classicist: once grant his canons of literary excellence, and his judgement is unerring. Cicero was, of course, more catholic in his tastes: he could enjoy Naevius and Ennius and Plautus and their like, and he felt himself the immediate heir of that straightforward, virile speech which Cato had preferred to the scholastic refinements of Greek rhetoric. Compared with this whole-hearted admiration for everything Roman, Quintilian's range is limited. For him Cicero and the great Augustans are supreme: Virgil is his Homer, Livy his Herodotus, Sallust his Thucydides, Cicero his Demosthenes and Plato. It is a good choice, but a student's choice; and it has become traditional among students. Greek classicism, it has been said, won its final victory in the schools of Greek literature during the reign of Augustus.[2] Quintilian is the first of the Latin classicists: he looks back to a past generation and

[1] *ibid.* i. 8, 12.

[2] Wilamowitz in *Hermes*, vol. xxxv (1900), pp. 41 foll.

is content with their achievement. He is a student writing for students; and it is characteristic of his theory that whilst Cicero recognizes the approval of a typical Roman crowd as the final test of good oratory,[1] Quintilian contrasts the judgement of 'the uneducated crowd' with the canons of his own more literary criticism.[2] Oratory has become a *doctrina scholastica*, to be relished by the cultured few: the younger Pliny, writing to Tacitus, justifies his own long-winded oratory by an appeal to the same rule. 'A short speech', he writes, 'is more popular with the many. Granted; but the many are lazy and it would be absurd to count their idle whims as a serious judgement.'[3] Was Tacitus wrong when he contended that oratory was dead in Rome?

Student though he was, Quintilian was a less well read man than Cicero; and here again he is typical of his generation. No reader of the younger Pliny's correspondence, with its artificial Ciceronianism, can fail to notice that the literary culture which Pliny affects is less humane (in the Latin sense of the word) than Cicero's spontaneous enthusiasm for philosophy and letters, for politics and the society of cultivated men. There is less of the old Roman vigour; and there is less of the new wine of Greek thought. It is the same with Quintilian. The *Institutio oratoria* is less vigorous than the *de Oratore*, and it is also less Greek. In theory, of course, Quintilian expects his ideal orator to be familiar with the best of both

[1] Cic. *de Or.* ii. 159; *Brut.* 184; *Or.* 24.

[2] Quint. x. 1, 43; see also ii. 12.

[3] Pliny, *Epp.* i. 20, 22.

literatures. The boy learns to speak Greek before he can speak Latin, begins his course of literature with the Greek *grammaticus,* and studies rhetoric in Greek as thoroughly as in Latin ; even in the tenth book Greek literature gets the preference. Yet it may fairly be questioned whether Quintilian or any of his contemporaries had the knowledge of Greek literature implied in Cicero's *politior humanitas.* They could read Greek, of course, speak it fluently and write it correctly. Quintilian names translation from Greek into Latin as a regular school-exercise ;[1] and the writers of this generation all affect the habit of using Greek phrases in the middle of their Latin. But it is worth while to test Quintilian's knowledge of Greek literature by the relative frequency of his quotations from the classical Greek writers. It is not a very sure test, for no writer is bound to quote all he knows ; and on the other hand, many of Quintilian's quotations may be taken at second-hand from one or other of the many text-books which he consulted when writing the *Institutio.* Nevertheless a rough estimate may be of interest, and yields surprising results.

The *Iliad* is quoted only fourteen times in the *Institutio oratoria,* and seven of these passages occur in a formal critique of Homer which is known to have been borrowed from a Greek source.[2] The *Odyssey* is quoted twice, once in the same formal critique.[3]

[1] Quint. x. 5, 2.

[2] *ibid.* viii. 4, 21, 24 ; ix. 3, 57 ; x. 1, 46–9 ; xi. 3, 158 ; xii. 10, 64.

[3] *ibid.* viii. 3, 84 ; x. 1, 48.

Hesiod, Aeschylus, and Sophocles do not appear at all: even Euripides, most quotable of all Greek poets, appears only twice, and one of the two passages quoted is certainly borrowed from Cicero's *de Oratore*.[1] Menander, whom Quintilian names after Homer as a poet to be read in the school of literature, and who is singled out for special praise in the tenth book,[2] appears twice.[3] Eupolis and Aristophanes are quoted in the chapter on music, which is again certainly dependent on some Greek source.[4] Pindar's authority is appealed to twice, and Quintilian seems to have known his poems well.[5] But no other Greek poet is quoted, and the figures for Greek prose literature are even more surprising. The *de Corona* of Demosthenes and its companion-piece by Aeschines are, of course, frequently cited as standard authorities,[6] and there are half-a-dozen passages from other speeches of Demosthenes.[7] But the other Greek orators do not appear at all, with the possible exception of Isocrates, two of whose panegyrics are cited in one passage as conventional types.[8] Plato's dialogues are well represented;[9] and there is an interesting chapter in which Quintilian shows detailed

[1] Quint. i. 12, 18 (=Cic. *de Or.* ii. 187); v. 10, 31.
[2] *ibid.* i. 8, 7; x. 1, 69–71. [3] *ibid.* iii. 11, 27; ix. 3, 89.
[4] *ibid.* i. 10, 18; cf. xii. 10, 65 (a commonplace of the schools).
[5] *ibid.* viii. 6, 71; x. 1, 109; cf. x. 1, 61.
[6] *ibid.* iii. 6, 3; iv. 2, 131; v. 13, 42 et saepe.
[7] *ibid.* iii. 8, 5, 65; v. 14, 4; vi. 1, 17; 5, 7; ix. 4, 63.
[8] *ibid.* iii. 8, 9.
[9] *ibid.* i. 10, 13; ii. 16, 3; 21, 4; iii. 1, 10–12; 4, 10; viii. 4, 23; 6, 64; ix. 4, 77; xi. 2, 9.

knowledge of the *Gorgias* and *Phaedrus*, though he complains that these two dialogues are usually quoted at second-hand by writers who have the reputation of being well informed.[1] The historians hardly appear at all. A sentence is quoted from Thucydides to illustrate the danger of falling into poetic rhythm, in the middle of prose ;[2] but the passage may well have been a stock example in Greek text-books of style. And there is one reference to Xenophon's *Memorabilia* :[3] nothing from the *Anabasis* or from Herodotus. Even within the strictest limits of classical selection the *lacunae* are numerous.

Statistics are seldom good evidence for anything so intangible as literary education ; but it should be remembered that Quintilian's subject-matter gave him endless opportunities for quotation, and that the *Institutio oratoria* fairly bristles with quotations from Cicero and Virgil. The conclusion is obvious. Quintilian's own reading was almost exclusively in Latin literature : the Greek poets and orators whom he quotes are those whom he had read and learnt by heart at school. Plato is the one prose author whom he seems to have read for the sheer delight of his literary style. Demosthenes and Aeschines were familiar from the ordinary routine of his classwork[4] —and the absence of quotations from the other Attic orators is thus doubly significant. With the exception of Demosthenes, Cicero has definitely displaced the Attic orators in the schools of Latin rhetoric :

[1] *ibid.* ii. 15, 5, 10, 24–31.
[2] *ibid.* ix. 4, 78. [3] *ibid.* ix. 2, 36. [4] *ibid.* x. 1, 22, 105.

Quintilian even boasts of the change.[1] As public professor of Latin rhetoric he could perhaps hardly have said less; but the contrast with Cicero's *humanitas* remains.

§ 5. *Vir bonus dicendi peritus.*

It is the fashion nowadays to explain every theory put forward by a Roman writer as the adaptation, or more often the misrepresentation, of some Greek ideal. Quintilian has a theory to put forward, an ideal in which he believes. For him only a good man can be an orator; perfect oratory implies a high moral standard as well as complete mastery over every form of speech. 'The orator whom we are educating', he says in his preface to the first book, 'is the perfect orator who can be no other than a good man; that is why we require of him not merely eminence in the art of speaking, but also every moral virtue.'[2] And again in the second book: 'The art which we are trying to teach and which we cherish as an ideal is a virtue, because it is that true rhetoric which belongs to the good man.'[3] And the twelfth book opens with these words: 'Let us assume that our orator is the man defined by Cato as "a good man able to speak"; but above all that he is what Cato puts first in his definition as being essentially the more important and noble, a good man.'[4] Language could not be plainer. Quintilian lays it down as a first principle of his whole educational

[1] Quint. x. 1, 105–12.
[2] *ibid.* i, *prooem.* 9, 18.
[3] *ibid.* ii. 20, 4.
[4] *ibid.* xii. 1, 1.

theory that only a good man can be an orator. Was his faith in this principle a personal conviction ? Or is he merely repeating the doctrine of some contemporary Greek teacher ?

One thing is certain : Quintilian did not get his ideal of the *vir bonus dicendi peritus* from Cicero. Once or twice in the *de Oratore* Cicero makes passing reference to the obvious truth that oratory can only benefit mankind if the orator is himself a good man. A man of talent, he says, should always be encouraged ; but if he is also a good man, he should be implored to perfect his gifts, for the sake of the State's welfare.[1] And later in the dialogue Crassus reminds his hearers that a gift for oratory carries with it a heavy responsibility, for eloquence is one of the noblest virtues : the greater our talent, the greater also should be our moral worth.[2] Quintilian goes far beyond this. For him it is literally true that a bad man can never be a good orator. That the gift of eloquence can be turned to evil purposes is, of course, obvious ; and Quintilian, were he forced to choose between talent and virtue, would prefer to see his pupil naturally dull rather than naturally wicked.[3] But true oratory is impossible without moral goodness. For the orator's aim is to carry conviction, and we trust those only whom we know to be worthy of our trust.[4] That is why Quintilian rejects as incomplete Cicero's definition of rhetoric : 'the art

[1] Cic. *de Or.* ii. 85. [2] *ibid.* iii. 55.

[3] Quint. i. 3, 2 ; xii. 1, 2.

[4] *ibid.* iv. 1, 7 ; 2, 125 ; vi. 2, 13 ; xii. 1, 10–13 ; Appel, p. 33.

of speaking so as to persuade '.[1] In one form or another that definition was taught in most of the Greek schools, and Quintilian quotes in support of it a long list of authorities: Plato (in the *Gorgias*), Aristotle,[2] Apollodorus, Hermagoras, Theodorus, and Cornelius Celsus. The last named, he complains, makes no secret of his view that eloquence is in no sense a virtue, having for its proper reward, not a good conscience, but victory in debate.[3] Quintilian protests against this cynical attitude. 'We have undertaken to educate the perfect orator, whom we wish to be above all a good man. Let us then turn rather to those who have a higher opinion of our labours.' And he ends by adopting the Stoic definition of rhetoric, 'the science of speaking well '.[4]

Does this mean that Quintilian borrowed his ideal of the *vir bonus dicendi peritus* from Stoic sources? Several recent critics have been tempted by this apparently simple solution.[5] One has even gone so far as to argue that Cato's famous definition could not possibly be original, but must be borrowed from the Stoa. 'What could have given the old man the idea of insisting so strongly on moral worth?'[6]

[1] Quint. ii. 15, 5; Appel, pp. 31 foll.

[2] For Quintilian's account of the definition given by Aristotle in his *Rhetoric*, see Angermann, p. 29.

[3] Quint. ii. 15, 32.

[4] *ibid*. ii. 15, 33–8.

[5] Raubenheimer, pp. 68 foll.; Appel, pp. 9 foll.; Schanz, ii. 2, p. 462.

[6] Radermacher in *Rhein. Mus*. liv (1899), pp. 285 foll., who there puts forward the view that the whole of Quintilian's twelfth book was an afterthought; later he modified these views (*ibid*. lvii (1902), pp. 312 foll.).

This is *Quellenkritik* run wild with a vengeance; but it is not the worst of its kind. Once allow that Quintilian has used Greek Stoic sources, and the *Quellenforscher* takes the bit between his teeth. Among the minor works attributed to Plutarch is a short essay *On the Education of Children*, which has often been compared with Quintilian's first book.[1] The two writings naturally have much in common, since both contain matter which was part of the ordinary stock-in-trade at the service of every essayist on the subject; and there were essayists in plenty under the early Empire. But the modern *Quellenforscher* sees 'parallels' everywhere, and the following gem deserves to be preserved.[2] Quintilian, writing for Latin-speaking parents, holds that a Roman boy should learn Greek before he can speak Latin: *a sermone Graeco puerum incipere malo.*[3] 'Pseudo-Plutarch', to give a dull writer an ugly name, insists that Greek boys should be taught to speak Greek correctly: ζητητέον . . . ἔτι μέντοι Ἑλληνικὰ καὶ περίτρανα λαλεῖν.[4] Why bother about the context? Down go the two 'parallels' in the *Quellenforscher's* note-book, and we have the proof that Quintilian and 'Pseudo-Plutarch' are both copying from some lost Greek source. Since Quintilian quotes Chrysippus five times in his first book,[5] the deduction is obvious: Quintilian and 'Pseudo-Plutarch' are both copying from Chrysippus, or

[1] Especially by Gudeman in his *Prolegomena* to the *Dialogus* of Tacitus.

[2] Raubenheimer, p. 56.

[3] Quint. i. 1, 12.

[4] Ps.-Plut., p. 4 A.

[5] Quint. i. 1, 4; 1, 16; 3, 14; 10, 32; 11, 17.

(better still) from some Stoic essayist who happens to quote Chrysippus in support of his own views.

Quintilian's own account of the debt which he owes to the writings of Greek philosophers is not quite so simple. Starting from his first assumption that only the good man can be an orator, he complains more than once in his *Institutio oratoria* that the philosophers have laid claim to more than their fair share in the work of education. Quintilian describes the history of this gradual usurpation in his preface to the first book, and the express mention of Cicero's name reminds us that he is here borrowing liberally from the *de Oratore*.[1] The same thought is repeated in the second book. 'Some maintain', he says, 'that it is the function of philosophy to discuss questions of ethical conduct; and I do not disagree with them. For by the word "philosopher" they mean "a good man"; and there is nothing surprising for us in the fact that an orator should also discuss these matters, since we do not distinguish between the orator and the good man.'[2] In the tenth book Quintilian includes the philosophers in his list of authors whom the young orator should read: 'we should not have to read them', he adds, 'if the orators had not abandoned to them the best part of their own work'.[3] And the twelfth book expresses the hope that 'some day a perfect orator may be given us who shall win back for eloquence

[1] Quint. i, *prooem.* 11–17; Cic. *de Or.* iii. 56–62.
[2] Quint. ii. 21, 12; Appel, pp. 9 foll.
[3] *ibid.* x. 1, 35; xii. 2, 6–8.

a stolen possession, and shall claim as his own this science, which is now made hateful by the arrogance of some who poison its good lessons by their own vicious lives.' [1]

These passages illustrate Quintilian's attitude towards the study of philosophy. With his interest in moral conduct he cannot deny the utility of much that the philosophers have written ; but in his eyes they are usurpers. And he is particularly hard on the modern philosopher *à la mode* of the early Empire. 'I have no difficulty in admitting that many of the ancient philosophers taught virtue and lived as they taught ; but in our own day most of those who make profession of philosophy have used the title as a cloak for the gravest crimes.' [2] The chapter on the study of jurisprudence ends with another shot at the philosophers.

> 'Some of those who find the labour of oratory too severe become lawyers. . . . Others are more arrogant in their sloth. All of a sudden they begin to frown and grow a beard, and pretend to despise the art of oratory. They go to school for a time with the philosophers, and then walk the streets in gloomy austerity whilst leading dissolute lives at home. Thus they acquire a reputation by despising others : for men can make a pretence of philosophy, but not of eloquence.' [3]

It is impossible to read this last passage without being reminded of Seneca. The style is Seneca's, and the thought is more akin to Seneca's than appears at first sight. Indeed there are many traces of

[1] *ibid.* xii. 2, 9.
[2] *ibid.* i, *prooem.* 15 ; Cic. *de Or.* iii. 57.
[3] Quint. xii. 3, 12.

Seneca's influence in the *Institutio oratoria*: most notable of all, the following personal reminiscence, which occurs in the tenth book.

'So far [we are at the end of Quintilian's list of Latin authors worth reading for their style], I have deliberately made no mention of Seneca, because of the false idea which people commonly have about me, that I condemn him and even hate him. The idea first gained currency when I was doing my best to recall our decadent, outworn, wilful style of oratory back to more exacting standards. Seneca was then almost the only author whom young men would read. It was never my intention to throw him aside completely, but I could not allow him to be preferred to better men whom he himself was never weary of attacking; for he knew that his own style was different, and felt that it could never please those who found pleasure in his predecessors. As for the younger generation, they enjoyed him but could not imitate him; they were as far behind him as he was behind the ancients. For I could wish that they were his equals or at least his near rivals. But they liked him for his faults, and made a point of affecting what they found easiest to imitate: thus they wronged Seneca by boasting that they had mastered his style.' [1]

And Quintilian ends with the advice that Seneca should be read only by those who are old enough to distinguish between his virtues and his faults: 'for there is much to admire in him, much that can be approved, provided you take the trouble to choose. If only he had done this himself! For a nature that so achieved its aim deserved to aim at better things.' [2]

There is a warmth of feeling in these regrets which suggests that Quintilian had once found himself under the charmer's spell. Seneca was at the height of his fame when Quintilian was a student in Rome,

[1] Quint. x. 1. 125–7. [2] *Ibid.* x. 1, 131.

and the young Spaniard must have read the *Dialogues* and the *Letters to Lucilius* when they were first given to the public. Did he owe them his interest in the psychology of education? I hardly think so; for Quintilian was born serious. Still he must have read his fellow-countryman's brilliant essays with a young man's enthusiasm, and the tone of the *Institutio oratoria* suggests that Quintilian owed more to these essays than to Cicero's philosophical dialogues. Indeed it is surprising how seldom Quintilian, who never misses an opportunity of quoting Cicero, takes a quotation from his hero's strictly philosophical work.[1] Seneca, on the other hand, is never quoted; and the omission is significant. The *Institutio oratoria* was written as an appeal from Seneca to Cicero, and Quintilian could hardly afford to make public his debt to the man whose influence he had been combating for the past twenty years.

Quintilian names the other Latin philosophers whom he thinks most worth reading: Brutus, Cornelius Celsus (a disciple of the Sextii), a Stoic writer by the name of Plautus, and Catius, an Epicurean.[2] But it is plain that none of these can be compared with either Cicero or Seneca. Plato was certainly Quintilian's favourite among the Greeks;[3] and he had also read Chrysippus.[4] These were, no doubt, the *veteres* whom he praises in his preface to the first book, but we have his own word for it that he had read others and did not consider himself

[1] See Bonnell's Index.
[2] Quint. x. 1, 123–4.
[3] *ibid.* i. 12, 15; x. 1, 81.
[4] See above, p. 193.

bound by the teaching of any particular school.[1] Further than this we can hardly go, and it is always a risky thing to deny the use of any individual writer. But Quintilian's general attitude towards the study of philosophy is plain enough. Granted the unhappy division between rhetoric and the theory of moral conduct, no orator can afford to neglect the works of the philosophers ; but he should read them with a view to oratory, not accepting the philosophic ideal. Quintilian would never have advised his young men to become pupils in the school of a philosopher. And it is interesting to note how carefully he abstains from giving this advice in the chapter of his twelfth book which deals expressly with the study of philosophy.

Virtue can be taught, so his argument begins. No man can hope to be just or brave or temperate who has not trained himself to acquire these virtues ; and his training will not be intelligent unless he makes a study of them.[2] But if all men must study the science of virtue, Cicero tells us that the orator has a peculiar need of this knowledge and must, therefore, study philosophy.[3] Cicero is again quoted a sentence or two further on, out of deference to his authority ; and then Quintilian's natural instinct asserts itself.

'It is not my purpose in giving this advice to persuade the orator to become a philosopher ; for no other profession has failed so conspicuously in the duties of a citizen and in every work proper to an orator. What philosopher was ever successful in the

[1] Quint. i, *prooem.* 11 ; iii. 1, 22 ; xii. 2, 26.
[2] *ibid.* xii. 2, 1–4.
[3] *ibid.* xii. 2, 5 ; Cic. *de Or.* iii. 74, 104.

law-courts or distinguished as a public speaker? Which of them ever took part in the government of his country, in spite of all their theories? My wish is that the orator whom I am educating should be, if possible, a Roman philosopher, showing himself a true citizen in practical work, not in private arguments. But since the study of wisdom has been abandoned by those who devote themselves to oratory, and has been withdrawn from its proper sphere—the forum with all its publicity—first to the porticoes and *gymnasia*, more recently to the privacy of the schoolroom; we must perforce seek those lessons which an orator must learn, and which are not given by teachers of rhetoric, from those who still retain the knowledge. We must read and re-read those authors who formulate the rules of virtue: only thus can the orator's life be combined with the knowledge of things divine and human.' [1]

There follows a long passage in which Quintilian enumerates the advantages to be gained from a study of each of the three philosophical sciences: dialectics, physics (including psychology), and ethics.[2] Here again the emphasis is on reading and private study, not on personal adherence to any particular school. The question of a choice between the different schools has to be faced, however, and Quintilian has a word to say about each. Epicurus professes contempt of rhetoric, Aristippus is too slothful, Pyrrho unable to make up his own mind: these three are immediately ruled out of court. The Academy is more useful because of the attention it gives to dialectics; and it can claim great orators (Cicero is not named) among its pupils. The Peripatetics were the first to debate *theses*, but Quintilian implies that he thinks poorly of their teaching. The Stoics, though

[1] Quint. xii. 2, 6–8.

[2] *ibid.* xii. 2, 10–23.

they lack style and fluency, are supreme in argument.[1]

'But the orator owes allegiance to no school. For the work to which he has set himself is nobler and more sublime; it is his aim to be recognized as perfect both in his oratory and in his life. The models which he must imitate are in speech those who are most eloquent and in moral conduct those who hold the strictest rule of honour and who point the straightest path to virtue.'[2]

The chapter ends with a characteristic phrase. All this study of philosophy is good and useful, but it is better and more useful to know the noble deeds of the past; the examples of courage, justice, good faith, temperance, and constancy left us by Fabricius, Regulus, Mucius, and their like. 'For the Greeks may excel in precept, but the Romans excel in what is greater, example.'[3]

It is tempting to go on quoting from this twelfth book, for it is full of characteristic sayings. Enough has been said, however, to show what Quintilian meant by his ideal of the *vir bonus dicendi peritus* and to define his attitude towards the schools of philosophy then fashionable in Rome. No hard and fast line can be drawn between Quintilian and Seneca—both were men of their time; but Quintilian's idealism was personal to himself. During his long career as teacher he had come to the conclusion that the decadence which all men recognized in Roman oratory was due as much to moral as to intellectual causes; and he set himself to the work of creating

[1] Quint. xii. 2, 24–5. [2] *ibid.* xii. 2, 26–7.
[3] *ibid.* xii. 2, 30.

a healthy reaction. He had fine gifts of literary appreciation, and he must have been a wonderful teacher; he was also a thoroughly good man. That he failed to revive the eloquence of a past generation is lamentably true: Pliny was his pupil, and that is evidence enough. But his criticisms of Latin poetry and prose are still readable and helpful; and his influence for good on the generation that knew him must have been very great. Pliny himself is as good a man as Quintilian, and there were no doubt others among his pupils. One name has a curious association. It was Juvenal who wrote: *Maxima debetur puero reverentia*[1]—words which cover all the teaching of Quintilian's first book, and recall Quintilian's insistence that at school the master holds the parent's place and should remember his responsibilities. Juvenal speaks of Quintilian with respect and (so far as dates go) may well have been his pupil. Was his *saeva indignatio* sometimes tempered by memories of one whose spirit was kindlier and more human in its sympathies?

[1] Juv. xiv. 47.

X

CONCLUSION

Quintilian's *Institutio oratoria* is a landmark in the history of Roman education: it is the culmination of a long development, and it had no successor. The later schools of the Roman Empire produced text-books of grammar and rhetoric in abundance; but no teacher was found who could speak with Quintilian's authority, no orator sufficiently interested in the theory of his art to produce a second *de Oratore*. There is only one possible exception. So much ink has been spilt in the discussion about the date and purpose of the *Dialogue on Orators* that one hesitates to name Tacitus as a critic of the *Institutio oratoria*. The two works are certainly connected in some way or other: no one who has read them both can doubt the fact. But what is the connexion? Was Tacitus a pupil of Quintilian, writing a criticism of his master's teaching years before the *Institutio oratoria* was published? Or is the *Dialogue on Orators* a polemical work, published shortly after the *Institutio*, in answer to Quintilian's defence of Ciceronianism? The question belongs properly to the history of Latin literature,[1] but a

[1] See especially Gudeman's *Prolegomena* to his second edition, where he defends the earlier date against most recent German scholars; Schanz, ii. 2, p. 294, who takes the opposite view; and Dienel in *Wiener Studien*, vol. xxxvii (1915), pp. 239–71.

word may be said as to the criticisms on contemporary education which the dialogue contains.

The two main personages in the dialogue, at least in its present fragmentary form, are Marcus Aper, the orator from Gaul, and Vipstanus Messalla. Aper's portrait, as drawn by Tacitus, is the portrait of a typical self-made man; proud of his success, frankly utilitarian in his principles and impatient of everything old-fashioned.[1] His principal speech is a brilliant rhetorical apologia for the rhetoric of the Silver Age.[2] Messalla, Aper's rival in the forum, takes the opposite point of view. Oratory in the Ciceronian sense of the word, he maintains, is dead:[3] and he analyses the causes of its disappearance. The old Roman tradition of home education has gone, and with it has gone all that was best in the Roman character.[4] Nowadays, the child is brought up in the midst of slaves, is spoilt by its parents in the nursery, and learns to talk about horses and gladiators and actors before it has learnt anything else.[5] And at school things are even worse: bad companions, weak masters, the wrong kind of lessons. In Cicero's day men studied history, philosophy, law, music, geometry, grammar, all the liberal arts: nowadays it is rhetoric, and nothing but rhetoric.[6] And rhetoric without a good general education will never produce an orator: for the orator must be able to talk well on any subject, before any audience. How can a man

[1] Tac. *Dial.* 2, 7–10. [2] *ibid.* 16–23. [3] *ibid.* 25–6.
[4] *ibid.* 28; see above, p. 14.
[5] *ibid.* 29. [6] *ibid.* 29–30.

speak about justice and honour and virtue and mercy unless he has studied philosophy ? How can he build an argument unless he has studied dialectics ? How can he discuss a legal case unless he has studied law ? [1]

At this point Messalla is interrupted for a moment and asked to explain in greater detail the kind of education he thinks suitable for an orator. In reply, he begins by describing the old Roman *tirocinium fori*, and the practical experience of an orator's work which it gave the student. In proof of his point he cites the names of four great orators—Crassus, Caesar, Pollio, and Calvus—who had won fame for themselves when barely twenty years old.[2] 'But nowadays', he goes on, using a phrase borrowed from the ceremonial *tirocinium fori* : 'our young men are brought (*deducuntur*) to the schools of rhetoric, which existed shortly before Cicero's day, but were closed by the censors Domitius and Crassus, in Cicero's phrase, as "schools of impudence". They are brought, I say, to these schools, where it would be hard to say whether the place itself or the students they meet or the kind of lessons they learn do them more harm.' [3] And he then launches out in a general attack on the schools of rhetoric, which breaks off suddenly in our mutilated text. What follows is an unsolved problem of literary criticism. There is a passage on the connexion between political disturbances and political oratory ; [4] another on the

[1] Tac. *Dial.* 31–2.
[2] *ibid.* 34.
[3] *ibid.* 35.
[4] *ibid.* 36–7.

contrast between the forum in Cicero's day and the forum under the Empire:[1] and a final passage on the change which good government has made in the Roman world.[2] There are now no orators, such is the conclusion to which Tacitus comes, because universal peace has made men happy, and has deprived the orators of their vocation.

Much of what Tacitus says is too rhetorical to be useful as evidence: but he is plainly right in his main contention. Political oratory as Cicero knew it was dead, and the Empire was responsible for its disappearance. But Messalla's speech raises a further question. How far was it possible to reconcile the ideals of Cicero's *de Oratore* with the changed conditions of Roman society? Quintilian's *Institutio oratoria* was a deliberate attempt to revive the Ciceronian ideal, in spite of all obstacles and in the face of discouragement. 'Let us strive after the best', such is Quintilian's last word of advice, 'and so doing we shall either reach the heights or at least see many beneath us.'[3] Tacitus ends his *Dialogue on Orators* with a parting shot, which has all the appearance of being written in answer to this idealism.

'Believe me, my good and (as far as we need it nowadays) eloquent friends, if you had been born in the good old days and they whom we admire had been born in this generation, or if some God had changed your lives and ages, you would have lacked none of their fame and glory as orators and they would have lacked none of your good sense and moderation. But since no man can have at one and the same time great fame and great

[1] *ibid.* 38–40. [2] *ibid.* 40–1.
[3] Quint. xii. 11, 30.

peace, let each man enjoy the good things of his age without reproach to the other.' [1]

Whether written before or after the *Institutio oratoria*, these words hint pretty plainly what Tacitus really thought of Quintilian's Ciceronianism. Which of the two was right, the historian or the schoolmaster? That is a problem which no student of Roman history can afford to ignore.

For the type of education which Quintilian describes in his *Institutio oratoria* remained for centuries the sole education known to the Graeco-Roman world. Poor men continued to send their children to the elementary schools of the *ludi magister* and the *calculator*; but the rich, the well-to-do and the professional classes sent their sons to the schools of literature and rhetoric, and were content with the 'liberal arts' of the ἐγκύκλιος παιδεία. 'The education of the ordinary man': that is what the phrase had originally meant, and its history shows that the 'encyclic' programme of studies was well adapted for its purpose. From the days of Isocrates and Aristotle to the fall of the Roman Empire no other form of education was known to Europe; and when the Church became the inheritor of Graeco-Roman civilization, she used the *artes liberales* as a convenient framework for the new Christian education taught in her schools. So long-lived a system of education must have been substantially good.

Yet the defects of the ἐγκύκλιος παιδεία are plain

[1] Tac. *Dial.* 41.

enough. The most obvious danger was that it tended to become a purely literary education, with facility in rhetorical composition as its ideal accomplishment. In Greece, where the national tradition of education was strong, this tendency was perhaps less marked, though it always existed: Hermagoras is a type of the ἐγκύκλιος παιδεία at its worst and narrowest. In Rome the tendency to subordinate the *artes liberales* to rhetoric was strong from the first. Cicero fought against it in his *de Oratore* and *Hortensius*; but the society for which he wrote ceased to exist within a generation of his death, and rhetoric carried all before it under the early Empire. Seneca is a born rhetorician, in spite of his philosophy, and Quintilian is not wholly free from the prevailing fashion: his *Institutio oratoria* makes rhetoric the centre of education to a degree which Cicero would never have tolerated. And the cult of rhetoric for its own sake was all the more dangerous in a society which had lost the tradition of political oratory. The talent which was devoted to the forum and the senate-house in Cicero's day had to content itself under the Empire with the professional law-courts or with an occasional oration before the senate in artificial surroundings. Oratory was soon perverted into rhetoric under these new conditions. Quintilian's cure for the trouble was a wide literary education in Greek and Latin; and no doubt he was right. In the old days oratory had formed itself under the stress of circumstances, and the speaker soon learnt to adapt his art to the requirements of his audience.

Now the audience was as often as not an artificial gathering of friends and critics, and the purpose of the new rhetoric was no longer to persuade, but to please. In other words the culture of Quintilian's contemporaries was a literary product, carefully formed on the best literary models, and content to be judged by literary standards: Cicero's *doctus orator* has become a *scholasticus*.

This narrowness of the ἐγκύκλιος παιδεία is shown in another aspect of Roman education. Greek tradition had always regarded the education of mind and body as two parts of one whole: μουσική and γυμναστική are co-relative terms. Rome never adopted this characteristically Greek ideal: the *artes liberales* had no connexion with bodily health. The old Roman tradition of healthy open-air exercise and of work on the farm was a thing of the past long before the advent of the Empire. Varro contrasts his own open-air life in the fields with more modern fashions,[1] and Horace's elaborate praises of Roman vigour and manhood are definitely an attempt to revive a forgotten past. Augustus was anxious to encourage Roman traditions of sport and physical exercise. He revived the *lusus Troiae*, in which young boys of noble family gave a public display of horsemanship and military prowess;[2] and he encouraged Virgil to describe in his *Aeneid* the sports and contests of early Italian tradition.[3] But the current of

[1] Varro, *apud* Non. 108, 24; see above, p. 18.

[2] Suet. *Oct.* 43; Barbagallo, p. 26.

[3] Virg. *Aen.* v. 548–603; vii. 160–5; ix. 603–20; Norden in *Neue Jahrb. für d. kl. Alt.* vol. vii (1901), p. 263.

fashion proved too strong for such artificial revivals of the past. The *lusus Troiae* came to an undignified end after ten or fifteen years, owing to the protests of Asinius Pollio, whose grandson had broken his leg in one of the manœuvres;[1] and half a century later Seneca speaks of the old Italian tradition as definitely belonging to the past.[2]

In Rome, at least, Greek athletics became fashionable under the Empire. Varro complains that every Roman villa must nowadays have its gymnasium;[3] and Strabo describes Greek athletics on the Campus Martius as one of the sights of Rome.[4] But the *palaestra* never got public recognition in Rome as part of a 'liberal' education: when we hear of it at all, it is usually in terms of reproach and even disgust. Cicero was openly contemptuous of Greek athletics;[5] Seneca and Lucan shared his contempt;[6] and the elder Pliny hated Greek athletes almost as much as he hated Greek doctors.[7] Tacitus even goes so far as to make Nero's interest in the *palaestra* a main charge in his attack on that Emperor's Government;[8] and it is significant that Caligula, Nero, and Domitian were the three Emperors most favourable to the new fashion.[9] Nerva reverted to

[1] Suet. *Oct.* 43. [2] Sen. *Epp.* 88, 19.

[3] Varro, *de Re rust.* ii. 1, 1; Friedlaender, ii, p. 150 (ii, p. 492).

[4] Strabo, v, p. 236.

[5] Cic. *de Rep.* iv. 4; *Tusc.* iv. 70; *de Or.* ii. 21: *de Off.* i. 130.

[6] Sen. *Epp.* 15, 1–4; 88, 18; Lucan, *Phars.* vii. 270.

[7] Pliny, *N. H.* xxix. 1–28; xxxv. 168.

[8] Tac. *Ann.* xiv. 15, 20, 21.

[9] Friedlaender, ii, pp. 145 foll. (ii, p. 484).

Roman traditions on this point, and a story told by the younger Pliny is characteristic of Roman opinion. Some unnamed benefactor had bequeathed a sum of money to the town of Vienne in Gaul to found an annual contest in Greek athletics. Trebonius Rufus, one of Nerva's friends, abolished the institution as a public nuisance, and an appeal was made to the Emperor against his action. Nerva upheld his friend's decision, and Pliny adds that one of the Emperor's most influential counsellors made the remark: 'I wish we could abolish the public games here in Rome.' [1]

Such unanimity of public opinion can only be explained by the existence of very real abuses. All the writers under the Empire point to the *palaestra* as the cause of grave moral scandals, and Plutarch, lover of all things Greek though he was, admits the charge.[2] And he adds a second criticism which is worth noting for the light it throws on Graeco-Roman civilization. The curse of professionalism had long since come upon Greek athletics, and Roman theorists were probably right in maintaining that the type of athletics taught in the *palaestra* developed the qualities of a professional athlete, but did not train the body for hard work.[3] That is a criticism which might also be made of the Greek schools of rhetoric. They taught men to declaim, but did not make them orators: or, as Seneca puts it, they educated 'for the class-room, not for life'.[4] Rome was the inheritor

[1] Plin. *Epp.* iv. 22.
[2] Plut. *Quaest. Rom.* 40.
[3] Plut. *loc. cit.*
[4] Sen. *Epp.* 106, 12.

of Greek civilization, but the civilization which she inherited had worn thin in the course of centuries.

And the process of wearing thin did not end with the fusion of Greek and Roman ideals in a Graeco-Roman culture. It was stayed for a century or so by the new impulse which the first contact of Greece and Rome gave to ancient thought; but it began again under the Empire, and continued steadily for the next four or five centuries. Cicero, Seneca, Quintilian, Fronto, Ausonius: these are names which suggest the successive stages of a gradual decline. They are not the only names which might be cited. But they are the names most typical of their age, and they are the names of men who owed what culture they had to the *artes liberales.* One name should perhaps be added to the list: Marcus Aurelius, the philosopher-Emperor. But the personality of this 'Stoic saint' suggests at once the most conspicuous want in all Graeco-Roman education. Apart from Quintilian's ideal of a *vir bonus dicendi peritus*—an ideal which might mean much or little, and which becomes increasingly vague and conventional in the writings of those later rhetoricians who quote the phrase at all [1]—the schools of literature and rhetoric under the Empire had no ideal of moral excellence to set before their students; for the lack of such an ideal they failed to invigorate the ancient world.

[1] Fronto, *ad Ver.* ii. 1 (p. 121, Naber); Fortunatian, Cassiodore, and Isidore (in Halm. *Rhet. Lat. Min.* i, p. 81; ii, pp. 495, 507); Boeth. *Comm.* περὶ ἑρμ., ii. 5, 11; Lehnert in *Philologus*, lix (1900), p. 577.

The old Roman traditions of civic virtue had once proved strong enough to put new life into Greek civilization, but the society which created and fostered those traditions had long since passed away. Much the same had happened in the Greek world, when Alexander's Empire broke down the barriers of the city-state. Greek Stoicism with its austere conception of philosophy had then supplied the need: it created a new ideal of moral excellence when the tradition of civic virtue failed. Rome produced no philosophy of her own, and was to the end distrustful of Greek philosophy. Marcus Aurelius is a lonely figure in Roman history, because he had the courage to believe whole-heartedly in the Greek Stoic ideal, and found in that ideal an inspiration which the *artes liberales* could never have given him. Yet the philosopher-Emperor has remained a lonely figure ever since. For a new world was growing up around him of which he was almost unaware, and that world found in the Christian faith a more satisfying ideal.

BIBLIOGRAPHY

(NOTE.—All works included in this Bibliography are quoted only by the author's name in the foot-notes, with the addition of a short title where there are two or more works by the same author.)

ANGERMANN, O. *De Aristotele rhetorum auctore*, Diss., Leipzig, 1904.

APPEL, B. *Das Bildungs- und Erziehungsideal Quintilians nach der Institutio Oratoria*, Donauwörth, Auer, 1914.

ARNIM, H. von. *Leben und Werke des Dio von Prusa*, Berlin, Weidmann, 1898.

BARBAGALLO, C. *Lo stato e l' istruzione pubblica nell' Impero Romano*, Catania, Battiato, 1911.

BELTRAMI, A. 'La composizione del libro duodecimo di Quintiliano' in *Studi italiani di fil. classica*, vol. xix (1912), pp. 63–72.

BLÜMNER, H. 'Die römischen Privataltertümer'. (*Handbuch Iwan-Müller*, iv. 2, 2), München, Beck, 1911.

BOISSIER, G. 'Comment les Romains ont connu l'humanité' in *Revue des deux mondes* (Dec. 1906–Jan. 1907).

Tacite (3rd edition), Paris, Hachette, 1908.

La Fin du Paganisme, 2 vols., Paris, Hachette, 1894.

BÖRNER, J. *De Quintiliani Institutionis Oratoriae Dispositione* (Pars Prior),[1] Diss., Leipzig, 1911.

BORNECQUE, H. *Les Déclamations et les déclamateurs d'après Sénèque le Père*, Lille, Siège de l'Université, 1902.

BREMER, F. *Die Rechtslehrer und Rechtsschulen im römischen Kaiserreich*, Berlin, Guttentag, 1868.

BROCK, D. *Studies in Fronto and his Age*, Cambridge, University Press, 1911.

CHRIST, W. *Geschichte der griechischen Literatur*, 2 vols. (*Handbuch Iwan-Müller*, vii, 6th edition), München, Beck, 1912–13.

COLSON, F. H. *M. Fabii Quintiliani Institutionis Oratoriae*, Liber I. Edited with Introduction and Commentary, Cambridge, University Press, 1924.

[1] The second part was never published.

COMPARETTI, D. *Vergil in the Middle Ages* (Eng. tr.), London, Swan & Sonnenschein, 1895.

DAREMBERG-SAGLIO. *Dictionnaire des Antiquités grecques et romaines*, 10 vols., Paris, Hachette, 1887–1919.

DIENEL, R. 'Quintilian und der Rednerdialog des Tacitus' in *Wiener Studien*, vol. xxxvii (1915), pp. 239–71.

DILL, S. *Roman Society from Nero to M. Aurelius*, London, Macmillan, 1904.

FIERVILLE, C. *M. F. Quintiliani de Institutione Oratoria liber primus* (with Prolegomena), Paris, Firmin-Didot, 1890.

FRANK, TENNEY. *Vergil: a Biography*, Oxford, Blackwell, 1922.

FREEMAN, K. *Schools of Hellas from 600 to 300 B.C.*, London, Macmillan, 1907.

FRIEDLAENDER, L. *Darstellungen aus der Sittengeschichte Roms* [1] (9th edition, revised by Georg Wissowa), 4 vols., Leipzig, Hirzel, 1919.

GARDTHAUSEN, V. *Augustus und seine Zeit*, 3 vols., Leipzig, Teubner, 1891–1904.

GERHÄUSSER, W. *Der Protreptikos des Poseidonios*, Diss, Heidelberg, 1912.

GIRARD, P. *L' ducation athénienne au Ve et au IVe siècle avant J.-C.* (2nd edition), Paris, Hachette, 1891.

GRASBERGER, L. *Erziehung und Unterricht im klassischen Altertum*, 4 vols., Würzburg, Stahel, 1864–81.

GUDEMAN, A. *P. Cornelii Taciti Dialogus de Oratoribus*, mit Prolegomena, &c. (2nd edition, in German), Leipzig, Teubner, 1914.

HIRZEL, R. *Der Dialog: ein literarhistorischer Versuch*, 2 vols., Leipzig, Hirzel, 1895.

JULLIEN, E. *Les Professeurs de littérature dans l'ancienne Rome et leur enseignement depuis l'origine jusqu'à la mort d'Auguste*, Paris, Leroux, 1885.

KOHL, R. *De scholasticarum declamationum argumentis ex historia petitis*, Diss., Paderborn, 1915.

KROLL, W. 'Studien über Ciceros Schrift de Oratore' in *Rhein. Mus.*, vol. lviii (1903), pp. 552–97.

[1] I have added (in brackets) the references according to the eighth edition (1910).

LAURAND, L. *De M. Tullii Ciceronis studiis rhetoricis*, Thesis, Paris, Picard, 1907.

LEO, FR. 'Quintilians kleine Deklamationen', in *Nachrichten der Gött. Ges. d. Wiss.*, ph.-hist. Klasse (1912), pp. 109–21.

LOTH, J. *Die pädagogischen Gedanken der institutio oratoria Quintilians*, Diss., Leipzig, 1898.

MARQUARDT-MAU. *Das Privatleben der Römer* (*Handbuch der röm. Altertümer*, Bd. 7), (2nd edition), Leipzig, 1886.

MARX, FR. *Incerti auctoris ad Herennium libri IV* (edidit cum prolegomenis), Leipzig, Teubner, 1894.

MÜLLER, I. von. *Die griechischen Privataltertümer* (*Handbuch Iwan-Müller*, v. 1, 2), München, Beck, 1893.

NETTLESHIP, H. *Essays in Latin Literature* (First Series), Oxford, Clarendon Press, 1885.

Lectures and Essays (Second Series), Oxford, Clarendon Press, 1895.

NORDEN, E. *Die antike Kunstprosa*, 2 vols., Leipzig, Teubner, 1898.

PAULY-WISSOWA. *Real-Encyclopädie der classischen Altertumswissenschaft* (in progress), Stuttgart, Metzler, 1894.

PETER, H. *Die geschichtliche Literatur über die römische Kaiserzeit bis Theodosius I. und ihre Quellen*, 2 vols., Leipzig, Teubner, 1897.

PRAECHTER, KARL. *Die griechisch-römische Popularphilosophie und die Erziehung*, Programm, Bruchsal, 1886.

RADERMACHER, L. 'Eine Schrift über den Redner als Quelle Quintilians und Ciceros' in *Rhein. Mus.*, vol. liv (1899), pp. 285–92.

RAUBENHEIMER, H. *Quintilianus quae debere videatur Stoicis popularibusque qui dicuntur philosophis*, Diss., Würzburg, 1911.

RITTER, C. *Die quintilianischen Deklamationen*, Tübingen, Mohr, 1881.

ROHDE, E. *Der griechische Roman und seine Vorläufer* (3rd edition), Leipzig, Breitkopf und Hartel, 1914.

SANDYS, J. *A History of Classical Scholarship*, vol. i (2nd edition), Cambridge, University Press, 1906.

SCALA, R. von. *Die Studien des Polybios*, vol. i,[1] Stuttgart, Kohlhammer, 1890.

[1] Vol. ii was never published.

SCHANZ, M. *Geschichte der römischen Literatur*, 6 vols. (*Handbuch Iwan-Müller*, viii, 3rd edition), München, Beck, 1907–19.

SCHMEKEL, A. *Die Philosophie der mittleren Stoa in ihrem geschichtlichen Zusammenhange*, Berlin, Weidmann, 1892.

SCHNEIDEWIN, M. *Die antike Humanität*, Berlin, Weidmann, 1897.

SEHLMEYER, FR. *Beziehungen zwischen Quintilians Institutiones Oratoriae und Ciceros rhetorischen Schriften*, Diss., Münster-i-W., 1912.

SPRENGER, J. *Quaestiones in rhetorum Romanorum declamationes iuridicae*, Diss., Halle, 1911.

SUSEMIHL, FR. *Geschichte der griechischen Literatur in der Alexandrinerzeit*, 2 vols., Leipzig, Teubner, 1891.

TEUFFEL, W. *Geschichte der römischen Literatur*, 3 vols. (6th edition), Leipzig, Teubner, 1910–16.

THIELE, G. *Hermagoras : ein Beitrag zur Geschichte der Rhetorik*, Strassburg, Trübner, 1893.

VOLKMANN, R. *Die Rhetorik der Griechen und der Römer* (*Handbuch Iwan-Müller*, ii. 3, 3rd edition), München, Beck, 1901.

WALDEN, J. *The Universities of Ancient Greece*, London, Routledge, 1913.

WALTZ, R. *Vie de Sénèque*, Paris, Perrin, 1909.

WARDE FOWLER, W. *Social Life at Rome in the Age of Cicero*, London, Macmillan, 1909.

Roman Essays and Interpretations, Oxford, Clarendon Press, 1920.

WILAMOWITZ-MOELLENDORFF, U. von. 'Asianismus und Atticismus' in *Hermes*, vol. xxxv (1900), pp. 1–52.

Platon : Leben und Werke, Berlin, Weidmann, 1919.

WILKINS, A. *Roman Education*, Cambridge, University Press, 1905.

WILLMANN, O. 'Aristoteles als Pädagog und Didaktiker' (*Die grossen Erzieher*, vol. ii), Berlin, Reuther-Reichard, 1909.

WORMSER, G. 'Le Dialogue des Orateurs et l'Institutio Oratoria' in *Revue de Philologie*, vol. xxxvi (1912), pp. 179–89.

ZELLER, E. *Die Philosophie der Griechen*, vol. iii, 1, 2 (4th edition), Leipzig, Reisland, 1903–9.

ZIEBARTH, E. *Aus dem griechischen Schulwesen : Eudemos von Milet und Verwandtes* (2nd edition), Leipzig, Teubner, 1914.

ZIELINSKI, TH. *Cicero im Wandel der Jahrhunderte* (3rd edition), Leipzig, Teubner, 1912.

I. INDEX RERUM

II. INDEX NOMINUM